HEARTS OF FIRE ...
Soldier Women of the Civil War
VOLUME I
With an Addendum on Female Reenactors

Author's Edition
by **LEE MIDDLETON**

HEARTS OF FIRE ... Soldier Women of the Civil War - VOLUME I

This is the first volume of an *on-going* work dedicated to collecting, identifying and documenting reports of women who served on the battlefields of the Civil War, with emphasis given to reports of women - both North and South - who went to war disguised as men. The author believes that this is the largest group compiled under one cover to date. Where possible, accounts have been quoted directly from reports made during the war years, with biographical data added when available. Includes illustrations, other daring acts of female bravery, a few items of human interest and concludes with an addendum of interviews with soldier women reenactors of the 1990's.

This collection is of vital historical significance, in addition to being interesting, poignant and sometimes amusing. No Civil War library would be complete without this volume. *A revised and expanded VOLUME II is currently in process. The author encourages input from anyone able to contribute to this project.* Send information or orders for additional copies to the author: Lee Middleton, P.O. Box 286, Torch, OH 45781

Compiled, Edited and Illustrated by Lee Middleton

(c) 1993 Lee Middleton

No portion of this book may be reproduced in any form for any purpose without prior written permission of the author.

LCCN # 93-78099
(ISBN # 1-882755-00-6)

1st Printing - Hardcover Author's Edition - May, 1993
2nd Printing - Hardcover Author's Edition - October, 1993

Printed by *Genealogy Publishing Service*, 448 Ruby Mine Road, Franklin, NC 28734 - USA

INDEX

ACKNOWLEDGEMENTS ... I-12
PREFACE ... I-14
FORWARD ... I-15
Soldiers' REGIMENT / STATE ... I-19
EPILOGUE ... 186
BIBLIOGRAPHY ... 187
REENACTORS' ADDENDUM ... 191
REENACTORS' INFORMATION ... 253

Amour ... 5
ANDERSON, Charlotte - aka: Charley ... *I-24*
Attempted Suicide ... 7
BAHR, Mrs. John ... 9
BARTON, Clara ... 11
Battled at Lookout Mountain ... 12
BAXLEY, Mrs. (see: *Prisoners*)
BEATTIE, Katie ... 12
BELL, Mary - aka: Tom Parker ... 13
BELL, Molly - aka: Bob Morgan/Martin ... 13
BLALOCK, Melinda - aka: Sam Blalock ... 14
"BLAND, Lieutenant" ... 15
"BLANK, James" ... 17
"BODLEY, Dr. John R." ... 19
BOIVERT, Madame (see: *Perkins*)
Bouncing Baby Boy ... 20
Bouncing Baby Boy (another) ... *I-23*
BOYD, Belle ... 22
Brave Housewife ... 23
Broad Passage ... 24
BROWN, Harriett - aka: Harry ... *I-19*

BROWN, Kate (see: *Prisoners*)
BROWNELL, Kady ... 26
BROWNLOW, Miss ... 29
BUDWIN, Florena ... 30
BURNS, Mary - aka : John Burns ... 30
CAMP, Fanny (see: *Taylor, Eliz.*)
CAMPBELL, Anna ... 31
"CANADIAN LOU" ... 31
Carroll Prison ... 31
CLALIN, Frances ... 33
CLAPP, Sarah E. ... 33
CLARKE, Amy/Annie - aka: Richard Anderson ... 33
CLAYTON, Mrs. ... 34
COLLIER, Madame ... 35
COLLINS, Sarah ... 35
COMPTON, Elizabeth /Lizzie ... 36
Confused ... 35
COOK, Lizzie - aka: William Ross ... 37
COOK, Maria ... 38
COOPER, Margaret ... 39
Copeland's Daughters ... 40
CORBIN, Mary ... 40
Corporal's Baby ... 42
COX, Lucy Ann ... 43
Crossley Reports ... 44
"Cruel War", The Ballad ... 1
CRYDER, Sophia ... 44
CUSHMAN, Pauline ... 46
CUSTIS, Mrs. ... 49
DAY, Frances - aka: Frank Mayne ... 50
DeHART, Jennie   (see: *Prisoners*)
DEMING, Mrs. L. ... *I-22*
DIVERS, Bridget ... 52
DUNBAR, Dora -and-
DUNBAR, Julia (see: *Prisoners*)

"DUTCH MARY" ... *I-21*
EDMONDS, Sarah (see: *Seeleye*)
ELLIS, Mrs. ... **53**
EMILY -?- ... **54**
ETHERIDGE, Anna ... **55**
EVERSOL, Sarah L. ... **57**
EWBANK, Hanna ... **59**
Family Resemblance ... **59**
FARNHAM, Amanda ... **60**
Fifty-ninth Ohio ... **60**
FINNAN, Elizabeth Cain ... **60**
FORD, Antonia ... **61**
Forty-ninth Georgia ... **61**
FOSTER, Augusta ... **61**
FOUR MORE (see: *"Frank Martin"*)
Fourteenth Iowa Suicide ... **62**
Freemantle's Report ... **62**
G____, Major ... **63**
G____, Mary J. ... **115**
GALLOWAY, Mary ... **64**
GAUSS, Lucy M. - aka: Bill Thompson ... **155**
GIBSON, Ella Hobart ... **64**
GOODRIDGE, Ellen ... **65**
GOODWIN, Victoria ... **66**
GOSHORN, Amanda -and-
GOSHORN, Belle (see: *Prisoners*)
Grant's Aunt ... **66**
GRAVES, Nellie (see: *F. Wilson)*
GREEN, Mary Jane (see: *Prisoners*)
GUERIN, Elsa Jane - aka: Lt. Charles Hatfield ... **68**
"H_____, Charley" ... **69**
HART, Nancy (also see: *Prisoners*) ... **70**
HAYS, Elizabeth (see: *Prisoners*)
HENRY, Margaret ... **71**
HERBERT, Ella ... **72**

HILL, Mary ... 72
HINSDALE, Jane ... *I-21*
HODGERS, Jennie - aka: Albert Cashier ... 74
HOLSTEIN, Anna ... 75
HOOK, Frances - aka: Frank Henderson/Miller ... 77
HORNE, Lucinda ... 80
HOWE, Kate W. - aka Tom Smith ... 80
HUGHES, Eliza C. (see: *Prisoners*)
HUNT, Emma ... 81
HUNTER, Mrs. ... 81
IBECKER, Elvira. - aka: Charles D. Fuller (see: *Day*)
JENKINS, Mary Owen (see: *Owens*)
"JOHEHOUS, Charles" ... 81
"Johnny" ... 82
JOHNSON, Mary Jane ... 84
JONES, Annie ... 85
JONES, Lizzie ... 85
K____, Nellie A. ... 87
KAMOO, Mrs. Abrev - aka: Tommy Kamoo ... 87
KATE __?__ ... 88
KENNEY, Lucy M. (See: *Thompson*)
Killed at Antietam ... 88
Killed in Pickett's Charge ... 89
Killed at Shiloh ... 90
KING, Josie ... 90
KIRBY, Mrs. Wm. ... *I-26*
Lady at Blue Licks ... 90
Leni Leoti, The ... *I-19*
LILLYBRIDGE, Annie ... 92
MADEMOISELLE Major ... 94
Many Women Served ... 94
MARCUM, Julia ... *I-20*
"MARTIN, Charles" ... 97
"MARTIN, Frank" ... 98
McCREARY, Mary ... *I-23*

McKENZIE, Marion - aka: Harry Fitzallen
  (also see: *Prisoners*) ... **102**
MILLER, Charley - aka: Edward O. Hamilton ... *I-23*
"MILLER, Frank" (see: *Hook*)
Minnesota Girl ... **103**
Mirrors and Silks ... **103**
Mission Accomplished ... **103**
MOORE, Madiline ... **105**
MUNDAY, Sue - aka: Lt.Flowers ... **105**
MURPHY, Maria   (see: *Prisoners*)
MURPHY, Mary Ann - aka: Samuel Hill ... *I-21*
"Nancies, The" ... **109**
New Orleans ... **110**
NILES, Elizabeth ... *I-22*
North Anna ... **110**
"NORTON, Charles" ... **111**
Ohio Girl ... **112**
OLDOM, Cornelia ... **113**
O'NEAL, Rose (Greenhow) ... **114**
One Hundred Fifty Recruits ... **115**
Orderly Sergeant's Baby ... *I-24*
OWENS, Mary - aka: John Evans ... **116**
PEPPERCORN, Melverina ... **117**
PERKINS, Mary Ann ... **117**
PETERMAN, Georgiana ... **118**
PETERSON, Belle ... **118**
PHELPS, Mrs. ... **118**
PHILIPS, Bettie Taylor ... **120**
PHILLIPS, Elizabeth   (see: *Prisoners*)
Pickett's Division ... **122**
PITTMAN, Mary Ann - aka: Lt.Rawley ... **122**
POLK, Antoinette ... **122**
POOLE, Ellie M. - aka: Stewart ... **123**
Popular girl ... **123**
PRATHER, Mary Jane   (see: *Prisoners*)

Prisoners ... **124**
Private Clapp's Girlfriend ... **125**
Provost Guard ... **126**
REMINGTON, Ida ... **127**
RENO, Ella (see: *Frank Martin*)
REYNOLDS, Major Belle ... **128**
"RILEY, William E." ... **129**
Sacramento, Ky ... **130**
"SALLIE" ... **130**
SANCHEZ, Lola ... **131**
SANSOM, Emma ... **132**
"SCHAFFER, Otto" ... *I-20*
SCHWARTZ, Miss ... **133**
SCOTT Sisters ... **134**
SEABERRY, Mary - aka: Charles Freeman ... *I-23*
SEELEYE, Sarah Emma (Edmonds) -
    aka: Franklin Thompson ... **136**
SEIZGLE, Mary ... **139**
Sheridan's Discovery ... **140**
SIMPSON, Mary - aka: Mary Timms ... **140**
SMITH, Alvira ... **142**
SMITH, Hanna -and-
SMITH, Joanna (see: *Prisoners*)
SMITH, Clarine "Kinnie" ... **144**
SMITH, Lydia ... **145**
SMITH, Mary ... *I-23*
SMITH, Sarah ... **146**
Southern Chivalry ... **146**
STERRITT, Mrs. ... **147**
SULLIVAN, Betsy ... **148**
SUMMERS, Mary (see: *Prisoners*)
TAYLOR, Elizabeth - aka: "Happy Ned" ... **149**
TAYLOR, Maria -and-
TAYLOR, Mattie ... **149**
TAYLOR, Sarah ... **150**

TEBE, Marie ... **153**
THOMAS, Vivia ... **153**
THOMPSON, Ellen ... *I-19*
THOMPSON, Lucy Matilda -
    aka: Bill Thompson ... **155**
Three Who Died ... **157**
"TOMMY" ... **157**
TOMPKINS, Sally ... **158**
TUBMAN, Harriet ... **159**
TURCHIN, Madame ... **160**
Two Prisoners from Georgia ... **161**
Two Tennessee Women ... **162**
VAN LEW, Elizabeth ... **163**
VELASQUEZ, Loreta - aka: Harry T. Buford ... **165**
"Vivandiere", defined ... **167**
WAKEMEN, Sarah Rosetta -
    aka: Lyons R./Edwin R. Wakeman ... **170**
WALKER, Mary ... **174**
Warrior River ... **177**
Who Was She? ... **177**
"WILLIAMS, Charles H." ... *I-20*
"WILLIAMS, John" ... *I-22*
WILLIAMS, Laura J. - aka: Henry Buford ... **177**
WILSON, Eliza. ... **178**
WILSON, Fanny ... **180**
WILSON, Maggie - aka: Charles Marshall ... **182**
WISE, Mary ... **183**
WITTENMEYER, Annie ... **183**
Women of Castroville, Texas ... **184**
Wounded at Chickamauga (see: *Hook*)
Wounded at Gettysburg ... **185**
Wounded Woman Yank ... **185**
WRIGHT, Mary (see: *Henry*)

ILLUSTRATIONS

Clara Barton, **10**
Battle of Carnifax Ferry, **I-18**
Belle Boyd, **21**
Kady Brownell, **25**
Miss Brownlow, **28**
Frances Clalin, **32**
Pauline Cushman, **45**
Bridgette Divers, **51**
Anna Etheridge, **55**
Family in Camp, **I-13**
Nellie Graves, **179**
Nancy Hart, **69**
Jennie Hodgers, **73**
Frances Hook, **76**
Mary Livermore, **3**
Madiline Moore, **104**
Belle Reynolds, **127**
Sarah Seeleye, **135**
Clarine Smith, **143**
Marie Tebe, **152**
Loreta Velasquez, **164**
Sarah Rosetta Wakeman, **169**
Mary Walker, **173**
Fannie Wilson, **179**

REENACTORS

BONEHAM, Emilie, **199**
BURGESS, Lauren Cook, **204**
CLAUDIO, Bernadette, **207**
COWSERT, Beth, **211**
DREWES, Dianne, **214**
EHLERT, Allison, **217**
HINDLE, Susan, **221**
HOFFMAN, Eleanor, **225**
KING, Wendy, **228**
RAINES, Sharon, **231**
SMITH, Sandra, **234**
STUART, Beth Anne, **236**
SUNSHINE, Cyndi, **239**
WILLIS, Patricia Anne, **245**
WISE, Catherine, **249**

ACKNOWLEDGEMENTS

My special thanks to **Lauren Cook Burgess**, Author/Reenactor, who donated her extensive research to this project and to author/researcher **DeAnne Blanton**, Military Reference Branch, National Archives, who not only made her research available, but has generously continued to donate advice and time assisting me in further research. For their interest, input, support, and encouragement I would also like to thank authors **Gregg Coco**, **Richard Hall**, **Kay Larson** and **Art Bergeron, Jr.**, Author/ Historian, LA Office of State Parks, as well as **Louise Arnold-Friend**, Reference Historian at the U.S. Army Military History Institute (USAMHI). I also extend my thanks to my good friends at the Farnsworth House in Gettysburg, **John Petersen** and **John and Patty O'Day,** to **Barb Lakin**, who opened her lovely home to us, and to all others who have taken such a generous interest in this project.

---**Lee Middleton (Urick)   1993**

For my husband, Gerry.

FAMILY IN CAMP

PREFACE

Prior to the last decade, only a handful of researchers have investigated elusive and scattered reports of women who fought in the Civil War disguised as men. More recently the subject has come to light as a very controversial matter - emphasized by today's modern women seeking to portray such women in reenacting and disputed by many who believe there were only a handful, or none at all.

Mary Livermore, in her book MY STORY OF THE WAR, estimates about 400 women in disguise as soldiers. She didn't say where this figure came from, but if it was from personal knowledge, that is astounding. If she, being only one person, had come across 400 ladies, how many more must there have been! My purpose for undertaking this continuing project was to identify and document *at least* 400 soldier women in disguise. After several years of research I feel this must may be only the *tip* of the iceberg.

Their trials, tribulations, and ways in which they kept themselves from being discovered to be females in the ranks will require more in-depth research than so far uncovered. Therefore, to get an idea of what it *may* have been like for them in the field, I have interviewed several women who reenact those roles today. It is a far cry, of course, from the real thing, but how can we *really* know unless we were there? Few of those ladies left us any personal memoirs. Certainly their daily survival conditions would be the same as the men with whom they served, but they must have had to deal with the additional and constant fear of discovery and subsequent exile, ridicule, and the more serious matter of possible physical abuse.

In this attempt to collect, identify and document the women disguised as men who infiltrated the camps for the purpose of serving on the battlefields of the Civil War, I have tried to compile data from the earliest sources available to me at the time, and have used direct quotes whenever possible (which may contain misspellings and undefined jargon.) The chance of duplication has not altogether been eliminated, as few sources state the same circumstances or facts (which would have made it easier to spot multiple accounts of the same person). However, when a duplication has been obvious, I have combined the data; where duplication is suspected, reference has been made to any other similar account. Because this research is slow and difficult, I have inserted for the sake of human interest, other incidental acts of female heroism bordering on combatant or battlefield association. - LM

FORWARD

At no time in the history of America, had women joined together in such numbers than at the outbreak of the Civil War. When some men were slow to respond, the Chicago Tribune (Apr./May 1862) reported that both Northern and Southern journals carried many accounts of eager women volunteering in their places.

No one expected the war to last more than three months. When it did, it created an extraordinary demand for any services women could render. They answered the call by becoming nurses, seamstresses, cooks, laundresses, teachers, sanitary workers, and contributed whatever talents they possessed. A nation of women alone, they were the sisters, wives, mothers, daughters and sweethearts of those who went to war. The efforts and memoirs of some of these gentle ladies on the home front have been recognized, highly appreciated, and widely publicized.

Some women who followed their men to war may have done so because survival without a man at home may have been nearly impossible as evidenced by the following letter from a Southern soldier's wife. The letter was produced as a defense for

Edward Cooper, who was being tried for desertion after being caught trying to get home to his family. (Unaccustomed to wartime conditions and procedures in this country, desertion was common; men felt they had the right to serve near their homes and be with their families when the army was inactive.) (26 p.101)

"My dear Edward: - I have always been proud of you, and since your connection with the Confederate army, I have been prouder of you than ever before. I would not have you do anything wrong for the world, but before God, Edward, unless you come home, we must die. Last night I was aroused by little Eddie's crying. I called and said 'What is the matter, Eddie?' and he said, 'O momma! I am so hungry.' and Lucy, Edward, your darling Lucy; she never complains, but she is growing thinner and thinner every day. And before God, Edward, unless you come home, we must die. Your Mary" - - Lee pardoned the young man. *(26 p.13)*

Some women ventured beyond the home front to follow the war performing camp services as vivandieres and assisting in the field hospitals as nurses. Officer's wives were given great freedom to follow their husbands, so there were often women and children in camp.

To differentiate between battlefield nurse, vivandiere, sutler, laundress, regimental daughter, is difficult. Regardless of what placed them on and near the battlefield in the first place, duties would eventually overlap out of necessity. Often in the thick of battle and under severe and adverse conditions - as in Clara Barton's situation - they paused only to wring out the heavy hems of their blood-soaked petticoats. Exhaustion, disease, and injuries caused many a premature death among these women. (30 p. 470, 527-531)

Yes, many matrons and young ladies took up sabre and pistol to ride into the fire for reasons that only they knew. Some reportedly went in search of excitement, some from fear of being left alone, some went out of a passion for country and cause and some out of a passion to be near the men they loved - whatever the cost. From both North and South, they went out as spies, mailriders, guerrillas, scouts, and saboteurs. (24 p.173)

Among these bold and adventurous women were those who cut their hair, donned male attire and fought in the ranks. Although other accounts have been intermingled here to give a more complete view of women's roles, the main context of my research has been to concentrate on gathering as many reports that I can find, about women who actually became, or tried to become, soldiers. Since there are many books by and about Civil War nurses, spies, and heroines in general, these reports have been kept to a minimum in this manuscript.

As you read the following brief accounts, allow yourself a moment to dwell on the circumstances that must have surrounded each episode and then consider the courage, time, planning and fortitude it must have taken to overcome the obstacles that presented themselves. What may seem ludicrous or foolhardy to us today, may have been the only recourse for those who were witnessing a war going on in their own back yards. Given a similar situation, what would you have done?

One who studies the Civil War is impelled by the tragedy, valor, and purpose of those who were there. Some call their interest a romance, some just call it research. But whatever it is called, it permeates the student with an unsettling, captivating, "*something*" that words have yet to adequately define.   LM   1993

BATTLE OF CARNIFAX FERRY

"BATTLE of CARNIFAX FERRY"
Sketched by Corp. Ned Roessler, Color Guard,
47th OV, Co., G. - 1861

NOTE: *Upon close comparison of clothing, etc., it is the author's opinion that three of the primary figures (encircled) in this sketch ..... are women.*

Soldiers' REGIMENT/STATE

*(Includes page numbers, alias, and cited references.
Names in bold and underlined disguised themselves as men.)*

GEORGIA:
49th   **Forty-ninth Georgia, 61** - Two Women *(43* p. 33-48);
            ("Letters to Amanda", Published letters home from Sgt. Maj.
            Marion Hill Fitzpatrick, 45th QA, Co. K, Thomas' Brigade"
            Raymond Rigdon, 1982)

ILLINOIS:
____   **Harriett Brown** - *"Harry"*, served three months [**]
____   **Mission Accomplished, 103** *(24* p. 524-25)
3rd   **Frances Hook, 77 -** *"Frank Henderson /Miller /Martin?"*
            (24 p. 172,567);*(Nat'l Tribune 29 Aug 1895)*
3rd Cav.   **Fanny Wilson, 180** *(24* p.170-71);*(20* p. 49);*(22* p. 80);
            (Frank Leslie's,7 Mar 1863)
3rd Cav.   **Nellie Graves, 180**   (same ref. as Fanny Wilson)
7th Cav.   Sarah E. Clapp, 33   Nurse *(1* p. 337-39)
17th, Co.A   Belle Reynolds, 128   Nurse *(15* p. 270);*(23* p. 94, 159-60, 376);
            (24 p. 268-69)
19th   Madame Turchin, 160 Officer's Wife *(16* p. 114-15);
            (23 p. 94); *(28* p. 853); (Anderson's "Story of the Ill.
            Central Lines During the CW", Ill. State Hist. Soc.)
19th   **Attempted Suicide, 7** *(16* p.113)
19th   *Frances Hook - (previously referenced)*
63rd   **Leni Leoti,** The Steamer - Female soldier discovered on board.
            (44 p. 201); [**]
65th   *Frances Hook - (previously referenced)*
90th   *Frances Hook - (previously referenced)*
95th, Co.G   **Jennie Hodgers, 74** - *"Albert Cashier"* (*1*); (*13* p. 111-12);
            (Washington Sunday Star, 29 Mar 1913);*(44* - Pittsfield IL
            Republican, 14 May 1913; "Pvt. Albert Cashier as Regarded by
            His/Her Comrades", Journal of the IL Hist. Soc., Summer 1988,
            p. 108-112);(O.R. Pen. File #C2 573 248)
116th   **Kate -?- , 88** *(41*); (Robertson's "Soldiers Blue and Gray",
            U of SC Press, 1988)
139th   **Ellen Thompson** [**]

INDIANA:
____   **Elizabeth Cain Finnan, 60** (Nat'l Tribune, 25 Jul 1907 - Obituary from
            Indianapolis News);(USAMHI Ref. # 2984)
____   **Woman in uniform** *arrested in Indianapolis* [**]
____ Cav.   **Emma Hunt, 81** (Military Images, May/Jun 1991, p. 24)
____ Cav.   **Wounded Woman Yank, 185** (*1*); (Anderson, ed.
            "The Shelley Papers", Ind. Mag. of History, XLIV,
            1948, p.186)
15th   *"William E. Riley", 129* *(Nat'l Tribune, Wash. DC, 25 May 1899)*
33rd   **Two Prisoners from Georgia, 161**   *(21* p. 65)
34th   **Mary Wise, 183**   *(22* p. 80)
66th   **Family Resemblance, 59**   *(44* - Owensboro KY Monitor, 20 Aug 1862)

[**(*44*)] - Further research in process for Vol. 2.

Intro - 19

IOWA:
- 2nd — *"Charles H. Williams"* - served with Lieutenant lover [**]
- 4th Cav. — **Elsa J. Guerin, 68** - *"Lt. Chas. Hatfield /Mountain Charley"* (*37*);(*44*)
- 14th — **Fourteenth Iowa Suicide, 62** (*43* p. 33-48)
- 27th — Two Tennessee Women, **162** - Heroines (*15* p. 499-500)

KANSAS:
- ____ — *"Otto Schaffer"*, A Butler County farmer and veteran in male disguise until her death [**]
- 5th — **Lizzie Cook, 37** - *"William Ross"* (*24* p. 204)

KENTUCKY:
- ____ — **Sue Monday, 105** - *"Lt. Flowers"*
  (*24* p. 296-87, 596-97)
- ____ — **Lady at Blue Licks, 90** (*24* p. 196-97)
- ____ — **Marion McKenzie, 102,125** - *"Harry Fitzallen"*
  (*14* p. 186); (O.R. Ser 2 Vol 5 p. 121-22);
  (Wheeling Intelligencer 25 Dec 1862, 20 Jan 1863);
  (Kaufman's "Under the Petticoat Flag", Southern Studies, Winter 1984)
- ____ — **Julia Marcum** [**]
- 1st Inf — **Sarah Collins, 35** (*18* p. 175);(*22* p. 80);(Kaufman's "Under the Petticoat Flag", So. Studies, Winter 1984);(*44* - Hurn's "Wisconsin Women in the War Between the States", Wisc. Hist. Comm., Original Papers #6, 1911, p. 103); (*44* - is this the same young lady who was discovered because of how she *put on her stockings?* Richardson's "The Secret Service, the Field")
- 4th — Bettie Taylor Phillips, **120** Nurse/Spy (*17* p. 122-24)
- 5th Cav. — **Ella Reno, 100** (Marvel's "Burnside", U of NC Press, 1991) (see 8th MI)
- 11th Cav. — **Elizabeth Compton, 36** (*6* p. 35-36);(*24* p. 605)
- 11th Cav. — **Mary Jane Johnson, 84** (USAMHI Ref. #652 -
  Journal entry of W.W. Sprague, 13th MA, Co. B, Belle Island Prison, 9 Dec 1863)
- 23rd Inf. — *"Frank Martin"*, **98** (see MI)

LOUISIANA:
- Wash. Art. of N/O — Mrs. John Bahr, Vivandiere (*2* p. 16,24);(*27* p.379);(*35* p. 21)
- ____ Cav — **Amy/Annie Clarke, 34** - *"Lt. Richard Anderson"* (*20* p. 49);(*22* p. 81); (Jackson Mississippian, 30 Dec 1862); (Simpkins & Patton's "Women of the Confederacy", NY 1936, p. 80);(Jackson's "The Southern Women of the Second American Revolution", Atlanta, 1863, p.7); (Kaufman's "Under the Petticoat Flag", So. Studies, Winter 1984);(DeFontaine's "Marginalia: or Gleanings from an Army Notebook", 1864, p. 113);*(44* - Cairo City Gazette, 25 Dec 1863; Darst's "Robert Hodges, Jr. - Confederate Soldier", E. Texas History Journal, Vol 9, #1, 1971, p. 37-38) **see TN**
- ____ Inf. — **Freemantle's Report, 62** (Freemantle's "Three Months in the Southern States", NY 1864, p. 173);
  (Kaufman's "Under the Petticoat Flag", So. Studies, Winter 1984); (Simkin & Patton's "Women of the Confederacy", NY, 1936)
- 21st — **Loreta Velasquez, 166** - *"Harry T. Buford"* (*9* p. 334-45);(*13* p. 675); (*27* p. 380-82); (Note similarity to *Laura J. Williams*, **177**)

MAINE:

___	**Augusta Foster, 61** (*23* p. 125)
5th	Amy Bradley - Nurse
7th	**Pvt. Clapp's Girlfriend, 125** (*24* p. 535)
13th	**Frances Clalin, 33** (ref. to this State in error?);
	(*5* p. 149); (Robertson's "Tenting Tonight", p. 27);
	(See *Mrs. Frances Louisa Clayton, 34, 13th MO Cav.*)
14th	**New Orleans, 110** (Gardner's "Recollections of the
	14th Maine Vol., Co. I, 1862-1865", p. 24)
17th	Dutch Mary, Vivandiere, who served w/husband [**]

MASSACHUSETTS:

6th	Lizzie Jones, 85 - Regimental Daughter (*2* p. 86);(*20*);(*24* p. 535-36)
53rd	**Mary Ann Murphy** - "*Samuel Hill*", served with her brother, Tom [**]
___	**Mrs. Abrev Kamoo, 87** - "*Tommy Kamoo*" (*10* p. 47);
	(Lancaster, PA Newspaper obituary - 1904,
	about her death in Boston)

MICHIGAN:

___	**Emily -?-, 54** - Drummer from Brooklyn, NY(*13* p. 205);(*30*) see NY
1st Cav.	Bridget Divers/Divens/Devens, 52 - Vivandiere (*2* p. 11);(*13*);(*16* p. 116-19);
	(*28* p. 241)
2nd	Anna Etheridge, 57 - Nurse (*2* p. 9);(*23* p. 113,370);(*28* p. 267);
	(*30* p. 470)
2nd	**Sarah (Emma Edmonds) Seeleye, 136** - "*Franklin Thompson*"
	(*7* p. 113-14,227,396);(*12*);(*13* p. 200);(*26* p. 149);
	(*29* p. 131);(Nat'l Arch. Pension Rec .#SC282,136);
	also see U. of MI Library and biography "She Rode with
	the Generals", Sylvia Dannett, Thomas Nelson & Sons,
	NY, 1960 and Sarah's autobiography, "Nurse and Spy")
2nd	**Jane Hinsdale** - served w/husband, Hiram T. (44 p. 198,202); [**]
3rd	Anna Etheridge (previously referenced)
5th	Anna Etheridge (previously referenced)
7th Cav.	**Mary Burns, 30** - "John Burns" (*22* p. 80);
	(Frank Leslie's Illustrated News, 19 Dec 1863);
	(New York Herald, 28 Dec 1863, 12,14; Aug 1864);
	(Hurn's "Wisconsin Women in the War",
	Madison, 1911 p. 103);(Detroit Adv. & Tribune, 25 Feb 1863)
8th	*Frances Hook (previously referenced in IL)*
8th	*Frances Hook (previously referenced)*
8th	*Ella Reno (previously referenced in KY)*
8th	**"Frank Martin", 98** - Bugler (*24* p. 622);(*30* p. 470);(*36* Vol. 2);
	(*40* p. 220-21);(*43* p. 42);(Seeleye's "Nurse and Spy");
	(see: Three Who Died, Frances Hook, Ella Reno, 2nd E. TN,
	25th MI);(44 - Robertson's "Michigan in the War",
	125th MI Regt. Hist., Lansing 1880) ; (see KY)
8th	*Ella Reno (previously referenced)*
10th	Mrs. L. Deming, Regimental Daughter [**]
21st	**Annie Lillybridge, 92** (*3* p. 442-43);(*24* p. 621)
25th	*"Frank Martin" (previously referenced)*
125th (?)	**Lizzie Compton, 36** (*36* Vol. 3- some confusion with
	Elizabeth Compton, 11th KY Cav.)

MINNESOTA:

Frances Louisa Clayton, 34 - from St. Paul -
(*44* p. 27-28,159,198,202; Wellsburg (WV) Herald, 9 Oct 1863; Cincinnati Gazette, 2 Oct 1863, taken from Grand Rapids Eagle); (Frank Leslie's 19 Dec 1863);(Quoted by Heisey, "Antique Week", 29 May 89);(NOTE: some similarities to *Frances Clalin, 33* -4th MO Cav.) [**]

Minnesota Girl, 103 (*22* p. 80)

MISSISSIPPI

Broad Passage, 24 - Capt., in uniform, but not disguise (*44*); (Lynchburg Virginian, 6 Oct 1864)

MISSOURI:

"**Canadian Lou", 31** (*1*)

4th, Co.I — *Frances Clalin, (previously referenced in ME)*
4th, Co.A — *Frances Clalin* (Cavalry) (" ")
6th — "**Charles Joehous", 81** (Nat'l Tribune, 13 May 1886)
13th, Co.A — *Frances Louisa Clayton (Clalin?)* (Cavalry) - (prev. referenced in MN)
15th — "**Sheridan's Discovery", 140** - Two Women (*23* p. 97)
17th, Co.H — "*John Williams*" found to be a female [**] (O.R., Nat'l Archives)

NEW JERSEY:

Mary Jane G----, 115 - was from Trenton (Independent Republican, Goshen, NY, 20 Jun 1864)

4th — **Elizabeth Niles,** served with husband, b. ca 1828, died aged 92 [**]
24th — *Nellie Graves (previously referenced in IL)*
24th — *Fannie Wilson* (" ")

NEW YORK:

see Michigan for "*Emily*" (drummer)
10th HA — **Sergeant**, had a baby boy [**]
11th — **Ida Remington, 127** (Detroit Adv. & Trib. 27 Aug 1863)
13th — **Maggie Wilson, 182** "*Charles Marshall*" _____
18th — **Charley Miller** - "*Edward O. Hamilton*", drummer, preferred male attire for life [**]
36th — (Six) _____
40th — Had a female **Lieutenant Colonel** [**]
41st — **Mary Seizgle, 139** (Moore's "Rebellion Record", Vol. 10, p. 87-2)
49th — Garibaldi Guard had six vivandieres dressed in red, blue and black [**]
102nd — **Nellie A. K----, 87** - 102nd NY (*22* p. 79);(*43*);("The Life of Pauline Cushman", Ferdinand L. Sarmiento, Keystone Pub., Phil., PA - 1866)
153rd, Co.G/H — **Sarah Rosetta Wakeman, 170** -"*Lyons/Edwin Wakeman*" (Burgess research into unpublished letters home. Enlistment recorded in "A Record of the Commissioned Officers, Non-Commissioned Officers and Privates of the Regiments which were Organized in the State of New York and Called into the Service of the United States to Assist in Supressing the Rebellion", 1866, Albany, NY, Weed Parsons & Co., Vol. 5, p. 354-55)

NO. CAROLINA:

18th, Co.D — **Lucy Thompson, 155** - *"Bill Thompson" (39)*;(Hoar's "The South's Last Boys in Gray", Bowling Green St. Univ. Press, 1986, p. 10-12);*(44* - Mull's "Profile of a Woman Veteran: The Life of Private Bill Thompson, Confederate States of America, Nat'l Women's Military Museum Newsletter, Vol. 1, #1, Spring, 1989; Crute's "Units of the Confederate States Army", Medlothian, VA, Derwent Books, 1987 (Hist. of 18th NC Inf.)

21st, Co.H — **Mary McCreary**, served with husband until she became pregnant [**]

26th, Co.F — **Malinda Blalock, 14** - *"Sam Blalock" (9 p. 334)*; *(22 p. 81)*;(Unpublished family history in the possession of descendant of Keith Blalock.); ("Histories of Several Regiments and Battalions from NC in the Great War", William Clark 1901, p. 330-31);("Bushwhackers", Wm. R. Trotter, Blair, Wiston Salem, 1988);("Confederate Women", Belle Wiley, p. 142);("Women of the Confederacy", Simkins and Patton, p. 80); (Fayetteville Observer, 29 Oct 1953)

OHIO:

3rd — **Ohio Girl, 112** *(24* p. 580)

41st — **Mary Smith,** enlisted to avenge brother's death gave herself away while she was wringing out a dishcloth [**]

52nd — Dr. Mary Walker, Surgeon *(2* p. 16, 18-19);*(8* p. 6-7); *(12)*;*(23* p. 380)

52nd, Co.A — **Mary Seaberry** - *"Charles Freeman"* quit after her gender was discovered [**]

59th — **"Fifty-Ninth Ohio", 60** Two women served three years.(36)

60th — **Charlotte Anderson** - *"Charley"* [**]

74th — Female **Orderly Sergeant** gives birth after 20 months of service *(44* -"James Greenalch Letters Home to Wife, Fedelia", Mich. History, Jun 1960, p. 237-38); [**]

89th — **Corbin, Mary, 40** (Col. Caleb Carleton Papers, 89th OH; Mss Div, Library of Congress. Extracted from letters to his wife, Sadie, dated 27 Aug 1863 and 15 Sep 1863.)

97th — Corbin, Mary (previously referenced)

OKLAHOMA:

— **Vivia Thomas, 153** *(38)*

PENNSYLVANIA:

— *"Charles Martin", 97* - *(24* p. 206) see Ibecker

9th Cav. — **Mary Owens , 116** *(Jenkins?)* - *" John Evans"* *(24* p. 161);*(22* p. 80);*(23* p. 94)

11th, Co.A — **Sophia Cryder, 44** ("The Training of an Army: Camp Curtin and the North's Civil War", Wm. J. Miller)

11th — "Sallie" - mascot dog

25th — (5) **"Five Soldiers"**

27th — Marie Tebe, **153** - Nurse/Vivandiere *(2* p. 6); *(28* p. 828)

46th, Co.D — **Elvira Ibecker, 50** - *"Charles D. Fuller/C. Norton/ C. Martin?* *(30* p. 470) see **Frances Day**

114th — Marie Tebe (previously referenced)

126th, Co.F — **Frances Day, 50** - *"Frank Mayne"* *(30* p. 470); ("A Sketch of the 126th Rgt. of PA Vol.", Lt. Col. D. Watson Rowe, 1869, Ted Alexander, ed.);("She Rode with Generals", Dannett, newsclipping on page following 161):("Regimental Losses in the Civil War", Wm. F. Fox, Albany, NY, 1889);*(44* - Nat'l

PENNSYLVANIA: (cont'd.)   .. **Frances Day**
Archives Official Roster for Co. F list Frank Mayne, 5th Sgt. deserted 24 Aug 1862; Ted Alexander, ed., "The 126th PA", Shippensburg, PA, Beidel Printing House, 1984)

141st   *"Charles Norton",* **111** (Craft's "History of the 141st PA Vol., 1862-1865 p.101-02) also see Ibecker

RHODE ISLAND:
1st   Kady Brownell, **26** - Color Bearer/Vivandiere
(*2* p. 5);(*4* p. 31-33);(*13* p. 82);(*23* p. 111, 119-20, 368-69); (*24* p. 268);(*29* p. 134-35);(*42* p. 24)

5th   Kady Brownell (previously referenced)
12th   *"Tommy",* **157** (*24* p. 193)

SO. CAROLINA:
14th Co. K   Lucinda Horne, **80** - Vivandiere (*27*) also (Chapman's "History of Edgefield County" p.483, 489-91)

TENNESSEE:
1st   Sarah Taylor, **150** - Capt./Regimental Daughter (*22* p. 85);(*24* p. 544)
1st, Co.K   Betsy Sullivan, **148** - Vivandiere (*27* p. 380)
2nd, E. Cav.   *Frances Hook (Frank Martin?) (previously referenced in IL)*
2nd, E. Cav.   *"Frank Martin" (previously referenced in MI)*
11th   *Amy/Annie Clarke* (previously referenced in LA)

_____   **Madame Collier, 35** Two Women (Ransom's "John Ransom's Andersonville Diary", 1881, reprinted by Berkeley Books, NY, 1988, p. 22)

_____   **Melverina Peppercorn, 117** (*32* p. 31); (Meriwether's "Recollections of 92 Years, 1824-1916", Nashville, 1956, p. 103-105, 161); (Kaufman's "Under the Petticoat Flag", So. Studies, Winter 1984*)*

_____   **Mary Ann Pittman, 122** - "*Lt. Rawley*" (*32* p. 30-31) O.R. Ser 2 Vol 7 p. 345-54

_____   *"Charley H ---",* **69** Died in U.S. General Hospital, Tullahoma, Spring 1865 (12 Aug 1882 report of Dr. J. A. Edison, 148th IL - USAMHI Ref. #57)

_____   **Margaret Henry, 71** - Imprisoned at Nashville (22, p. 81-82)
   Mary Wright, 71 - Imprisoned at Nashville (22 p. 81-82)

VERMONT
_____   **Amanda Colburn Farnham, 60** - Fron St. Johnsbury, VT (23 p. 186)

VIRGINIA:
13th   Lucy Ann Cox, **43** - Vivandiere (*22* p. 85)

[W] VIRGINIA:
5th Cav.   *Marion McKenzie* (previously referenced in KY)
_____   **Prather, Mary Jane, 125** (*14* p. 188) O.R. Ser 2 Vol 5 p. 547-48
_____   **Summers, Mary, 125** (14 p. 188) O.R. Ser 2 Vol 5 p. 547-48
_____   **Hays, Elizabeth, 125** (Wheeling Intelligencer, 14 May 1863); (O.R. Ser 2 Vol 5 p. 547-48, Ltr from Wm. Hoffman to Major Darr)

WISCONSIN:

___	Belle Peterson, 118 (See Hurn's "Wisconsin Women in the War")
___	Ellen Goodridge, 65 (*15* p. 532-33);(*44*)
	also see Minerva Quarterly, Spring, 1990, p. 41, Larson's "Bonny Yank and Ginny Reb"
1st HA	Ella Hobart Gibson, 64 - Chaplain (*22* p. 86); (*1* p. 337-339)
	also see New York Herald, 18 Sep 1865 and O.R. Pensions File # W3370, Nat'l Archives
5th	Eliza Wilson, 178 - Nurse/Vivandiere (*20* p. 49);(*22* p. 85)
	see also Hurn's "Wisconsin Women in the War", p. 100
7th	Georgiana Peterman, 118 (*16* p. 119);(*23* p. 95)
	also see Wheelwright's "Amazons and Military Maids", Pandora Press, London, 1898, p. 94;
	(Plattville, WI, "*WITNESS*", Mar 1864)
7th	Hanna Ewbank, 59 - Regimental Daughter
	see Hurn's "Wisconsin Women in the War"

MISCELLANEOUS: (As far as my research has progressed, these women were in disguise unless otherwise noted.)

Anderson, Charlotte - *"Charley"*, I-24 (*44* p. 197-203); [**]
Battled at Lookout Mountain, 12 - Two Women (*36*);(*43* p. 41)
Bell, Mary , 13 - *"Tom Parker"* (*22* p. 84);(Richmond Examiner, 31 Oct & 25 Nov 1864);
        (Robertson's "Tenting Tonight", p. 61);
        (Robertson's "Soldiers Blue and Gray", U. of SC Press, 1988)
Bell, Molly, 13 - *"Bob Morgan/Martin"* (same as sister, Mary)
"Bland, Lieutenant", 15 (*3* p. 169-71)
"Blank, James", 17 (USAMHI ref # 1016) Nat'l Tribune, 25 Feb 1892);
"Bodley, Dr. John R.", 19 (*10* p. 26)
Bouncing Baby Boy, 20 - Officer/Prisoner, Johnson Island, (*22* p. 84);
        (Sandusky, OH Register, 12 Dec 1864);
        (Wiley's, "Confederate Women")
Bouncing Baby Boy, (another), I-23 [**]
Broad Passage, 24 - Officer (*44*)
Brown, Harriet, I-19 - *"Harry"* (*44* p. 197); [**]
Budwin, Florena, 30 (*13* p. 86);(*38*)
Camp, Fanny, 149 - (*43* p. 42)
Carrol Prison, 31 (Burgess - Unpublished letters home, in descendants' possession)
Confused, 35 [*44*]
Corporal's Baby, 42 - Corporal, 10th MA (*3*);(Yankee Magazine, Jun 1961)
"Crossley Reports", 44 ("Henry Besancon Papers", Mss Dep., Perkins Library, Duke Univ.,
        Ltr dated 26 May 1864);(A. Jackson Crossley to S. Bradbury,
        HQ Army of the Potomac, 29 May 1864, Duke Univ.
        Library);(Wheelright's "Amazons and Military Maids", 1989)
Deming, Mrs. L, I-22 (*44* p. 198); [**]
"Dutch Mary", I-21 (*44* p. 17, 201); [**]
Ford, Antonia, 61 - Lieutenant CSA (Nat'l Trib. 25 Feb, 3 Mar 1932)
Four More, 100 - one Lieutenant (*24* p. 622);(*40*)
Galloway, Mary, 64 (Clara Barton, "Work and Incidents", ms Lecture, n.d., ca 1866);
        ("An Army Surgeon's Story", St. Louis, IL Mag. 24, No. 50,
        Apr 1883, p. 137-50);("Clara Barton, Professional Angel",
        Eliz. Brown Pryor, U. of PA Press, Phil. 1987, p. 99)

Hays, Elizabeth, 125 (Wheeling Intelligencer, 14 May 1863);(O.R. Ser 2 Vol 5 p. 547-48, Ltr from Wm. Hoffman to Major Darr)

Howe, Kate W., 80 - *"Tom Smith"*, (National Tribune 10 Sep, 29 Oct, 26 Nov, 10 Dec 1885);(USAMHI Ref. #4729)

Jenkins, Mary Owen, 116 (see: Owens - Ref. in PA);(*44* p. 144,201)

"Johnny", **82** (Nat'l Tribune 25 Sep 1884);(USAMHI Ref # 193)

Killed at Antietam, 88 (Seeleye's, "Nurse and Spy")

Killed in Pickett's Charge, 89 (*10* p. 40);(O.R., Report of Gen. Hays on Gettysburg Burials - contained conf. note, "woman found killed during the ... charge -- with husband.");("High Tide at Gettysburg", Glen Tucker);(*44* - Gettysburg Times & News, 1927, p. 18; Grim & Roy's "Human Interest Stories of the Three Days of Battles at Gettysburg")

Killed at Shiloh, 90 (*13* p. 14);(44 - Brooks' "Shiloh Mystery Woman", CW Times Illus., Aug 1978, p. 29)

Kirby, Mrs. Wm., I-26 (44 p. 198); [**]

"Madamoiselle Major", **94** (*29* p. 397-98) - in officer's uniform, but not as a man.(*44* - Coyningham's "Sherman's March Through the South", Sheldon & Co., NY, 1865, p. 194-97)

Many Women Served, 96 (USAMHI Ref. #4635)

Julia Marcum, I-20 (*44* p. 199); [**]

McCreary, Mary, I-23 [**]

Miller, Charley, I-23 - *"Edward O. Hamilton"* [**]

Mirrors and Silks, 103 ("Civil War Memories of Mrs. Adeline Deaderick", Anna Mary Moon, ed., Tennessee Hist. Quarterly, 7 Mar 1948, p. 58); (Kaufman's "Under the Petticoat Flag", So. Studies, Winter 1984)

Madiline Moore, 105 (*42* p. 24)

Niles, Elizabeth, I-22 [**]

North Anna, 110 (*33* p. 245);(see "Crossley Reports")

One Hundred Fifty Recruits, 115 (see Mary Jane G___);(Independent Republican, Goshen, NY, 20 Jun 1864)

Orderly Sergeant's Baby, I-24 [**]

Pickett's Division, 122 (*32* p. 31)

"Schaffer, Otto" **I-20** [**]

Seaberry, Mary, I-23 - *"Charles Freeman"* [**]

Smith, Mary, I-23 [**]

Summers, Mary, 125 O.R. Ser 2 Vol 5 p. 547-48

Taylor, Elizabeth, 149 - *"Happy Ned"* (*43*)

Thompson, Ellen, I-19 [**]

Three Who Died, 157 (*36*);(Hoar's "The South's Last Boys in Gray")

Who Was She?, 177 (USAMHI Ref. #2337)

"Williams, Charles H.", **I-20** [**]

Williams, Laura J., 177 - *"Henry Buford"* (*32* p. 30);(Kaufman's "Under the Petticoat Flag", So. Studies, Winter 1984);(DeFontaine's "Marginalia", 1864 p. 65-66)

Wounded at Chickmauga, 184 (*5* p. 149);(Wittenmyer's "Under the Guns", Stillings & Co., Boston 1885)

Wounded at Gettysburg, 185 - Two Women (*10* p. 40);(Letter of Thomas Read, Co. E, 5th MI, 20 Aug 1863, U. of MI Library.

THE CRUEL WAR

The cruel war is raging, Johnny has to fight
Oh, I want to be with him, morning till night
I want to be with him, it grieves my heart so

"Won't you let me go with you?"
"No, my love, no."

Today it is Sunday, Monday is the day
Your Captain will call you, and you must obey
Your Captain will call you, and you will have to go

"Won't you let me go with you?"
"No, my love, no."

I'll tie back my hair, men's clothing I'll put on
I'll pass as your comrade as we march along
I'll pass as your comrade. No one will ever know.

"Won't you let me go with you?"
"No, my love, no."

Oh Johnny, dear Johnny, I feel you are unkind
For I love you far better than all of mankind
I love you far better than words can e'r express

"Won't you let me go with you?"
"Yes, my love, yes."

(Ballad Recorded by Peter, Paul, and Mary)

*****

"Who has fully narrated the consecrated and organized work of women, who strengthen the sinews of the nation with their unflagging enthusiasm, and bridged over the chasm between civil and military life, by infusing homogeneousness of feeling into the army and the people, keeping the men in the field civilians, and making the people at home, of both sexes, half soldiers?"
– MARY LIVERMORE - 1887

Mary Ashton Rice Livermore 1820-1905

A teacher and the wife of a minister, Mary was one of the founders of the Sanitary Commission in the Chicago area. Covering the 1860 election as an editor, she became increasingly disappointed in the government's provisions for the troops. Already a reform activist, in 1862 she became national director of the Commission and travelled the country lecturing and organizing more chapters. After the war, she wrote, "<u>My Story of the War: A Woman's Narrative of Four Years Personal Experience</u>", and continued her work for women's suffrage. (13 p. 390)

MARY LIVERMORE

(Author's Note: The following account, though lengthy and over-embellished, has been added as an example of what some young ladies may have envisioned prior to their running off after a dashing young sergeant. What is interesting here, is that the bride (semi-military) and groom are both in uniform.)

AMOUR

(A Wedding in Camp)

Six bold riflemen clad in blue, with scarlet doublets over the left shoulder, bearing blazing torches; six glittering Zouaves, with brilliant trappings, sparkling in the light; and then the hollow square, where march the bridegroom and bride; then seven rows of six groomsmen in a row, all armed cap-a-pie, with burnished weapons, flashing back the lustre of the Zouave uniform; and all around the grand regiment darkening the white tent folds, as their ruddy faces are but half disclosed between the red and yellow glare of the fires, and the soft silver light of the May-moon.

(This is all, you will bear in mind, out on the broad, open air. The encampment occupies a conically shaped hill-top, flanked around the rear crescent by a wood of fan-leaved maples sprinkled with blossoming dogberries, and looking out at the cone upon the river swards below. The plain is full of mounds and ridges, save where it bulges in the centre to a circular elevation perfectly flat, around which, like facades about a court-yard, are arrayed the spiral tents, illuminated in honor of the coming nuptials.)

The bride is the daughter of the regiment; the to-be-husband a favorite sergeant. Marching thus, preceded by two files of sixes, and followed by the glittering rows of groomsmen, the little cortege has moved out of the great tent on the edge of the circle, and comes slowly, amid the bold strains of the grand "Midsummer Night's Dream," toward the regimental chaplain.

You have seen the colored prints of Jenny Lind on the back of the music of "Vive la France." You have noted the light-flowing hair, the soft Swiss eye, the military bodice, the coquettish red skirt, and the pretty buskined feet and ankles underneath. The print is not unlike the bride. She was fair-haired, blue-eyed, rosy-cheeked, darkened in their hue by exposure to the sun, in just the dress worn by les filles du regiment.

She was formed in that athletic mould which distinguishes the Amazon from her opposite extreme of frailty. You could not doubt her capacity to undergo the fatigues and hardships of a campaign, but your mind did not suggest to your eye those grosser and more masculine qualities which, whilst girting the woman with strength, disrobe her of the purer, more effeminate traits of body.

You saw before you a young girl, apparently about eighteen years of age, with clear, courageous eye, quiverless lip, and soldierly tread - a veritable daughter of the regiment.

You have seen Caroline Richings and good old Peter (St. !) march over the stage as the corporal and la fille. Well, this girl, barring the light flaxen hair, would remind you of the latter drilling a squad of grenadiers.

The bridegroom was of the same sanguine, Germanic temperament as the bride. As he marched, full six feet in height, with long, light colored beard, high cheek-bones, aquiline nose, piercing, deeply-studied blue eye, broad shoulders, long arms, sturdy legs, feet and hands of laborious development, cocked hat with blue plume, dark blue frock, with bright scarlet blanket, tartan fashion over the shoulder, small sword, you would have taken him for a hero of Sir Walter.

Faith, had Sir Walter seen him, he himself would have taken him. In default, however, of Sir Walter, I make bold to appropriate him as a hero on the present occasion. Indeed, he was a hero, and looked it, every inch of him, leading that self sacrificing girl up to the regimental chaplain, with his robe, and surplice, and great book, amid the stare of a thousand anxious eyes, to the music of glorious old Mendelssohn, and the beating of a thousand earnest hearts!

The music ceased; a silence as calm as the silent moon held the strange, wild place; the fires seemed to sparkle less noisily in reverence; and a little white cloud paused in its course across the sky to look down on the group below; breathing of the spectators, and the vague burning of the fagot heaps; a few short words, a few heartfelt prayers, the formal legal ceremonial, and the happy "Amen".

It was done. The pair were man and wife. In rain or sunshine, joy or sorrow, for weal or woe, bone of one bone, and flesh of one flesh, forever and ever, amen! ~~Quoted (3)

ATTEMPTED SUICIDE
(Soldier - 19th Ill.)

"I remember an occurrence of that afternoon when we visited the camp of the 19th Ill. I was watching companies that were drilling, a good deal amused at their awkwardness and their slow comprehension of the orders given them. One of the Captains came to me, with an apology for intrusion, and begged to know if I noticed anything peculiar in the appearance of one of the men, whom he indicated.

It was evident at a glance that the "man" was a young woman in male attire, and I said so. "That is the rumor, and that is my suspicion," was his reply. The seeming soldier was called from the ranks and informed of the suspicions afloat, and asked the truth of them. There was a scene in an instant. Clutching the officer by the arm, and speaking in tones of passionate entreaty, she begged him not to expose her, but to allow her to retain her disguise. Her husband had enlisted in his company, she said, and it would kill her if he marched without her.

"Let me go with you!" I heard her plead.
"Oh, sir, let me go with you!"

She was quietly conducted outside the camp, when I took her in charge. I wished to take her to my home; but she leaped suddenly from the carriage before we were half way from the camp, and in a moment was lost amid the crowds hastening home from their day's work. That night she leaped into the Chicago river, but was rescued by a policeman, who took her to the Home of the Friendless. Here I found her, a few days later, when I made an official visit to the institution. She was extremely dejected, and could not be comforted. It was impossible to turn her from her purpose to follow her husband.

"I have only my husband in all the world," she said, "and when he enlisted he promised that I should go with him; and that was why I put on his clothes and enlisted in the same regiment. And go with him I will, in spite of everybody."

The regiment was ordered to Cairo, and the poor woman disappeared from the Home the same night. None of us doubted but she left to carry out her purpose. " ~~Quoted (16)
---Mary Livermore (1887)

MRS. JOHN BAHR
aka She-Bear
(Vivandiere-Wash. Art. of New Orleans)

Mrs. Bahr served alongside her husband and performed many camp duties as a Vivandiere, as well as assisting in the hospital. Her colorful uniform was provided by Colonel Slocomb himself.

Undaunted, she was found tireless in tending to the needs of the soldiers, as a mother would care for her children. She and Mr. Bahr were much loved and respected earning them the affectionate names of "he bear" and "she bear." (24)

CLARA BARTON

CLARA BARTON
(Battlefield Nurse)

When the war broke out, Clara was unmarried and working as a clerk in the patent office. Had this tragic event never occurred, the world may never have known this mighty little woman. However, bored and restless, she seized this opportunity to put her boundless energy and intelligence to greater service, thus making her eternal mark on the history of this country.

Wasting no time, she sharpened her shooting skills until she could put "...nine balls successively within the space of six inches at a distance of fifty feet..." Clara's tiny five foot frame appeared on many of the bloodiest battlefields in the midst of shot and shell to give comfort and assistance to the sick, wounded and dying. Following McClellan to Antietam, with only two assistants, she traveled through Maryland three days and nights, loading her wagon with supplies along the way, and sleeping among them at night. She reached Burnside's corps the night before the battle. Fearlessly the next morning, she followed an artillery train onto the battle site. Grateful surgeons, their medical supplies exhausted and reduced to using corn husks for bandages, provided twenty five men to assist her in administering to the soldiers.(23),(7)

BATTLED AT LOOKOUT MOUNTAIN
(Two Soldiers-U.S.A.)

There were at least two women involved in this battle, one of whom was killed in the fight. The other woman, from Illinois, acted as a scout in the reconnoitering of Gen. Bragg's troops. She also served Gen. Blair's 17th, as an attache.(36)

KATIE BEATTIE
(Saboteur - C.S.A..)

Katie was well-known and respected in the South by military leaders for her skills as a spy, smuggler and saboteur. She torched warehouses and Federal boats and successfully affected the escape of many prisoners.

Eventually, however, she and her landlady were arrested and imprisoned for their deeds. (22)

MARY and MOLLY BELL
aka Tom Parker and Bob Morgan/Martin
(Soldiers- Virginia, "Early's Veterans")

The *Richmond Examiner*, 31 October and 25 November, 1864, recounts the dubious activities of the sisters Mary and Molly Bell.

Mary and Molly had been successful in concealing their feminine identities for two years before being discovered in the fall of 1864 and sent home to Pulaski County by Gen. Early by way of Richmond and Castle Thunder.

They were accused of being common camp followers of questionable morals. Perhaps they were - perhaps they weren't. But upon being sent home, still in their uniforms, they were "perfectly disconsolate at being separated from their male companions in arms." (22)

MALINDA/MAUDE BLALOCK
aka Sam Blalock
(Soldier - 26th NC, Co. F)

In the mountains of Western North Carolina, Malinda and her husband, Keith, were notorious as "bushwhackers". They enlisted together in May of 1862, with Malinda posing as her husband's brother (uncle?), "Sam".

Secretly, Keith was a Union sympathizer and refused to enroll unless he could take his wife with him. Recruiter Moore finally agreed to keep Malinda's true identity a secret. He enrolled them both, whereupon they drilled and carried out their soldierly duties. They participated in three engagements, in the hope they'd get close enough to Yankee lines to desert. However, when Keith fell ill, (*family legend says he rubbed himself down with sumac to cause a rash*) Malinda revealed her identity and was discharged with her husband. (9),(22)

Family legend further states that Malinda had to "disrobe" to prove she was a girl, and that it was Col. Vance who released her from service. Malinda was SARAH MALINDA PRITCHARD, daughter of William Alfred and Elizabeth GRAGG Pritchard. Malinda was the granddaughter of the Revolutionary War's William Gragg. Malinda died young, and Keith re-married. They were from the Watauga Co., NC area.

FIRST LT. BLAND
(Officer, CSA)

"I was officer of the guard, on as bright a July day as ever dawned on creation; and though it was oppressively warm, as early as guard mounting, eight o'clock, yet that interesting ceremony had passed off magnificently, and I was preparing to go the ground rounds immediately after the call for the second relief, when Lieutenant H., the old officer of the guard, sent his respects, with an earnest request for me to call on him at his marquee for special consultation.

'H--l is brewing at post number twelve,' said he, as he took me by the hand, 'and this fellow will tell you what he saw there; and you may rely upon trouble there before tomorrow.' 'An' I saw nothing at all, at all, but a ghost sure,' said the Irish soldier; 'it came out of the hill forenent (?) the old graveyard, shook its fist at me as it passed, and went into the bush towards the fort.'

"'How did it look?' inquired H.
"'Look? indade, how should it look, but like a woman draped in white, with eyes of fire?'

"An hour after, I was carefully searching the ground in the vicinity of post number twelve, when my ears were saluted with the well-known cry of, 'Buy any pies 'n' cakes? -- all clean and new; twenty-five cents for the pies, two cakes for a penny.'

"'Where is your pass, my good lady, if you are a camp follower; and why are you here among the rocks and bushes, if you wish to sell your marketing?' said G.

"'I am the honest wife of Pat Maloney, of the fourteenth Maryland, and stopped here to rest me weary limbs after coming five miles down from me home in the hill, your honor!'

"'Very likely,' said I; 'but will you please march down to the camp, and submit to a slight inspection of your basket and papers, if you have any.'

"'I have no papers, sir; and why should you put a loyal woman, and a wife of a Union soldier, to this trouble, bad luck till ye?'

"' You will not be harmed, madam. If you are a loyal woman, as you say, you will be the propriety of so doing.'

"Cakes and pies, sure enough, but no papers; and I began to believe that there was no connection between her and Pat's 'ghost;' but why should she wear a pair of men's boots?

"'Och, these were the boots me husband wore before he 'listed, sure!'

"And so the captain, somewhat given to gallantry, volunteered to accompany her to her friends, two miles toward her 'home in the hill,' where she was to give positive proof that she was 'neither a spy nor a ghost.' And away they went, a single soldier only accompanying them, amid the ill-suppressed laughter of the regiment.

"Noon, one o'clock, two o'clock, and no tidings of the captain! What was to be done? A squadron of cavalry was ordered to dash up the hill, reconnoiter, and report. And then time wore heavily away for an hour, when the cavalry charged into camp and up to headquarters, when instantly the long roll was beat, and in five minutes the regiment was under arms in line of battle. A perfect silence ensured, and the adjutant read the following note:

"`Colonel D.: I am willing to exchange the pies, cakes and basket for the soldier and the d----d fool captain whom I caught with crinoline. Peddlers and ghosts are at a premium in these parts just now.*
Yours, in HASTE,
BLAND, First Lieutenant C.S.A.'

"The soldier's musket was found four miles from camp, with the note from the WOMAN LIEUTENANT sticking on the point of the bayonet; and so the captain was captured."
~~Quoted (3)

"JAMES BLANK"
(Soldier, C.S.A)

The following account appeared in the *National Tribune*, Wash. D. C., Feb. 25, 1892, as told by M. Quad of the *Detroit Free Press*. (It is not clear whether or not this is a fictional account.)

"We had crossed the river to hunt for Lee and give him battle in the Wilderness. Darkness was just settling down, and the advance had halted for the night, when a squad of cavalry brought in a young man from our front. He wore a mixed uniform, as did most of the Confederates at that day, or as did most of those belonging to the partisan commands. He had on blue trousers, a butternut jacket and a hat that belonged to either side.

They said he was a spy. They said it carelessly enough, but there was an awful significance in the term at that hour. In camp he would have been searched, interrogated and imprisoned. It might have been weeks before his trial, and he would have been allowed every chance for his life.

We were on the march. There had been fighting. There would be more to-morrow. That meant a drumhead trial for the spy.

How speedily everything was arranged. I was at headquarters and saw and heard it all. Within half an hour a court-martial was convened -- grave-faced officers who looked into the face of the young man at first with interest -- then with something like admiration. I said a young man. I was wrong. He was a boy of 17 or 18. He had big blue eyes, chestnut curls and his cheeks were as smooth as a girl's. He was a handsome lad, and I believe that every man in the tent felt to pity him.

"What's your name?"
"James Blank."
"What regiment?" No reply.
"Are you a citizen or soldier?"
No reply.
"Can you make any defense to the charge
of being spy?"
No reply.

The officers looked at each other and nodded, and the president waved his hand. It didn't seem a minute before a file of soldiers came. The face of the boy grew white, but he moved like one in a dream. His big blue eyes looked upon one after another, as if searching for a friend, and my heart yearned to cry out that he was only a boy and ought to be given more time.

Tramp! Tramp! Tramp! It was the detail marching him off into the darkness.

"Halt! Tie this handkerchief over his eyes!"

They had brought a lantern. By its light I saw the big blue eyes for the last time as they looked around in a dazed way. I wanted to shout to the boy and warn him that it was not even yet too late to prove that he was not what they believed him to be, but the grimness of the scene parched my tongue.

"Place him there! Fall back! Attention.
Ready - aim - fire."

Ten minutes later the officer in charge of the firing party touched his cap and reported: *"Orders have been executed, sir!"*
"Any further evidence?"
"No sir, except that she was a young woman!"

~~~~~~

"DR. JOHN R. BODLEY"
(at Gettysburg)

Did the Confederates have a woman doctor in service at Gettysburg? If so, it is truly one of the most carefully kept secrets of that conflict. And even though the services of Dr. Mary Walker, a Union surgeon who worked with the wounded here, are not so well known, the presence of a Rebel woman surgeon is even more astounding. Here is how Lizzie R. (Plank) Beard got suspicious.

"Here is a true story of the happenings on the (Edward Plank) farm about three miles west of Gettysburg, situated on the west bank of Willoughby's Run. The house is a large brick. ..the family consisted of three small children, the parents, and an uncle. On July 1, we were told, 'This house will be a hospital and you can expect many wounded men here.'

"At this hospital, there were two Doctors, one a very well built man of fine personality. (His) name cannot be recalled. The other - John R. Bodley of Georgia - was a smaller man of kind disposition and bore the many characteristics of a woman, and was often spoken of, by the family as 'the Woman Doctor.' These two doctors were constant companions.

One winter I read in one of the New England papers of a woman, I can't recall her name, and the story in full of her enlisting and being in the service during the Battle of Gettysburg. I don't say John R. Bodley was this woman, but this clipping goes a long way to prove that there was a woman doing service after the Battle at a Gettysburg hospital." ~~Quoted (10)

BOUNCING BABY BOY
(Officer's Son - C.S.A.)

On Dec. 12, 1864, the *Sandusky Ohio Register* reported that a baby boy had been born to a female officer in the Confederate army who was imprisoned at Johnson Island.

Further in this article it was reported that there were *many reports* of Union women as soldiers, but that this was the first the editors had heard reported of a Confederate woman soldier.

BELLE BOYD

BELLE BOYD
(Spy - C.S.A.)

Belle was one of the most clever, beautiful and famous of all female Civil War spies and much has been written about her adventures. She rarely disguised her beauty, but used it to her favor by adorning herself with wide skirts, jaunty hats and luxurious hair. Not opposed, however, to donning a boy's attire to ensure safe passage through the lines, Belle once raced her mount, "Fleeta" over fifty-four miles of mountainous terrain to deliver to Jackson at Luray, a packet of papers stolen from a Federal officer's pocket during a lover's kiss.

Born in Martinsburg, [W] Virginia in May, 1844, she was a brilliant student, attending the Mount Washington Female Seminary at the age of twelve. Elegant Belle made her debut in Washington society in 1860.

In 1861 she visited her first Southern camp at Harpers Ferry. For whatever reasons resulting from her visit to that camp, Belle became a spy at only seventeen years of age. It was also that same year, she shot and killed a Federal soldier for assailing her mother while her father was away with the Confederate army.

In her escapades, Belle was captured and imprisoned many times. But on August 15, 1864 she married Mr. Hardinge, a Federal officer who deserted his cause for the love of Belle. Upon his untimely death, however, Belle took up the acting profession.

Later on, Belle married a second and yet a third time before her death in 1900, at Kilbourne, Wisconsin, while on a stage tour. (19),(28),(29)

THE BRAVE HOUSEWIFE
(Heroine-23rd KY)

In the fall of 1862, when Bragg and Kirby Smith made their swift and inglorious retreat from Kentucky through Cumberland Gap, they were sharply pursued by Rousseau. One morning the regiment in the van, the 23rd Kentucky, when about twenty-five miles east of Wildcat Mountain, were greatly surprised to see a squad of ragged Confederates come filing slowly into camp disarmed, and a woman walking behind them with a musket in her hands. There were eleven of the Confederates, and the woman handed them over to the Colonel as prisoners of war.

She said they came to her house the night previous, and finding that her husband was a volunteer in the Union lines, proceeded to help themselves promiscuously to everything they fancied. Some ran down the chickens, and began to kill and eat, while others cut up her carpets for horse blankets, and committed wanton depredations about the house.

The incensed woman remained quiet, but watched her opportunity. Presently they were all collected in the largest room, and making merry over the fire, having left their muskets in a stack near the door. Weary, and suspecting no mischief in a solitary woman, they relaxed their watch, while she quietly removed all the fire-arms but two loaded muskets, which she took in her hands, and standing by the door, demanded a surrender.

One of them, more alert than the rest, made a spring for the muskets, but fell dead on the floor with a ball through his body. She told them quietly that any further attempt to escape would be met by a similar fate. As they had a resolute foe to deal with, discretion now became the better part of valor: they submitted to the fortunes of war, and at daylight she marched them into the Union camp. ~~Quoted (15)

BROAD PASSAGE

The Charlotte North Carolina Times reported the sighting of a beautiful female Confederate Captain from Mississippi, aboard the train to Richmond. It was obvious by her medals of valor that she had participated in some serious battles. Her elegant, black-belted uniform was topped off by a straw hat trimmed in golden buttons. (44)

KADY BROWNELL

KADY BROWNELL
(Vivandiere- Daughter of the Regiment)
1st/5th Rhode Island, Co.H

One of the Civil War's most beloved daughters, was Kady Brownell, who enlisted in the 1st RI with her husband Robert, only a few days after their marriage. They later re-enlisted in the 5th R.I.

Born Kady McKensie in Caffaria, South Africa in December 1842, she was the daughter of a Scottish born soldier in the British Army, Angus McKensie and his wife Alice. In April 1861, while living in Providence, RI, she married a mechanic named Robert Brownell.

Kady's skills with weapons soon earned her respect as one of the most accurate marksmen in the regiment, and she was highly praised by Burnside. Though always well armed, and attired in the "coast uniform", she elected to bear into battle the regimental colors for her company of sharpshooters. In the fiercest of battles, her uniform often covered with blood from her fallen comrades, Kady saved many a life by standing by the colors as a point toward which the men could rally, and running out in front when the Fifth was mistaken as Rebel forces and were about to be fired upon. She was known to have carried the colors at Fairfax Court House, Roanoke Island and Bull Run.

Never was her bravery so evident however, than at the Battle of New Bern. Not only had she carried her own regimental colors, but when the standard bearer of the Sixth regiment fell, she recovered it and carried it across the field, receiving a flesh wound herself. Her trophy, which she brought home with her from battle, was a highly prized Secessia rifle.

And never was her patience and kind heart tested more than in this same battle when a wounded Rebel soldier, whom she'd moved out of the mud and attempted to comfort, shook his fist and cursed at her. Insulted, her immediate reaction was to plunge a bayonet toward his chest. The blow having been thwarted by a wounded Union soldier laying nearby, however, caused Kady to repent and spare the Rebel's life.

Kady and Robert were in many battles, but when Robert's fighting days were ended by receiving a wound which fractured his thigh bone in the battle of New Bern, she laid down her standard and stayed by his side until he was discharged in the fall of 1863. They returned to Providence, and eventually Robert assumed the duties as custodian of the Jumel Mansion in New York. When Robert died, Kady replaced him in that position.

Clinton Scollard wrote a poem about Kady, some lines from which follow here:

> *"While the mad rout at Manassas was*
> *surging,*
> *When those around her fled wildly, or*
> *fell,*
> *And the bold Beauregard onward was*
> *urging,*
> *Who so undaunted as*
> *Kady Brownell!"*

(2),(4),(13),(23),(24),(29)

MISS BROWNLOW

MISS BROWNLOW
(Heroine)

The house of the celebrated, bold-hearted and out-spoken Parson Brownlow was, at one time, the only one in Knoxville over which the Stars and Stripes were floating. According to arrangement, two armed secessionists went at six o'clock one morning to summarily haul down said [banner]. Miss Brownlow, a brilliant young lady of twenty-three, saw them on the piazza and stepped out and demanded their business.

"We have come to take down them stars and stripes." She instantly drew a revolver from her side, and presenting it, said -- *"Go on! I'm good for one of you, and I think for both!"*

"By the look of that girl's eye she'll shoot," one remarked: "I think we'd better not try it; we'll go back and get more men," said the other.

"Go and get more men," said the noble lady; *"get more men and come and take it down, if you dare!"*

They returned with a company of ninety armed men, and demanded that the flag should be hauled down. But on discovering that the house was filled with men armed to their teeth, who would rather die as dearly as possible than see their country's flag dishonored, the secessionists retired.   ~~Quoted (24)

FLORENA BUDWIN
(Soldier - U.S.A.)

Florena joined the army (disguised as a man) with her husband, a Pennsylvania Artillery Captain, and was able to remain undetected throughout her service. Neither was her sex revealed upon her capture and imprisonment at Andersonville, where her husband met his death. Florena remained in confinement until the Union forces threatened to overtake the prison, resulting in the prisoners being moved to a location in Florence, SC. She remained at the prison to help nurse the sick, but when an epidemic threatened her life, the failing Florena was at last discovered by doctors.

Upon realizing she was a woman, she was given special accommodations and care. All in vain, however, Florena died Jan. 25, 1865, and is buried at Florence, SC National Cemetery. (13),(38)

MARY BURNS
(Soldier - 7th MI Cav)

The *Detroit Advertiser and Tribune* of Feb. 25, 1863, recounts the incident that a woman named Mary Burns, disguised as a soldier in uniform, was arrested in Detroit and not permitted to depart with her company. (22)

ANNA CAMPBELL
(Courier)

Mrs. Campbell, a Unionist in Northern Alabama, once rode seventy miles in thirty six hours to carry information to General Streight. ~~Quoted (22)

"CANADIAN LOU"
(Soldier -Missouri Rgt.)

The *Memphis Bulletin*, Dec. 19, 1862, reported:

"A woman formerly extensively known in this city as "Canadian Lou", was arrested in this city last night dressed in men's clothes. She was put in jail for inebriety. She was with a Missouri regiment on its recent march from this city to Holly Springs and back." ~~Quoted (1)

CARROLL PRISON
(Soldier)

Sarah Wakeman, whose account appears later in this manuscript, wrote home to her family in August or September of 1863, that she'd discovered a woman imprisoned in Carroll prison, Washington, for serving as a Major in the Union army.

Her unpublished letters also mention two Confederate female spies also in prison there.

FRANCES CLALIN

FRANCES CLALIN
aka -?-
(Soldier - 13th ME, 4th MO)

Although Frances is mentioned in many accounts and her photos widely published, very little is known about her.

In uniform as a Cavalry trooper, she is believed to have also served in the Missouri militia. A period inscription on back of a photograph of Frances L. CLATIN (in uniform) indicates that she may have served in the 4th MO heavy artillery, in Co. I, for 13 months, and in the cavalry unit, Co. A for 22 months. (Info courtesy Andrew German, Mystic, CT., 1992) (NOTE: See MRS. CLAYTON - could be the same.)

SARAH E. CLAPP
(Battlefield Nurse - 17th IL Cav.)

During the Civil war, a few women were recognized officially by the military without having to conceal their sex. One of them was Sarah, a commissioned nurse. (1)

AMY/ANNIE CLARKE
aka Richard Anderson
(Lieutenant - LA Cav./11th Ten.)

On Dec. 30, 1862, the *Jackson Mississippian* reported that brave Amy enlisted in the Confederate army to be near her husband, Walter. Although she served seven months in a Louisiana cavalry first, she finally was able to join him in the 11th TN Infantry. She was by his side at Shiloh when he was killed. Wounded herself, she buried him with her own hands.

Amy continued to fight however, and was wounded a second time, which led to her capture at Richmond, KY. Her true identity discovered, she was given a dress and sent back to Confederate lines. Born in Iuka, TN, the last time Amy was seen, she was in Jackson, Mississippi and planning to re-enlist.(20) (22)

MRS. FRANCES LOUISA CLAYTON (Clalin?)
(Soldier - 13th MO Cav.)

Frank Leslie's Illustrated Newspaper of December 19, 1863, and other reports of the time, gave the account of a young woman from St. Paul who married a Mr. Clayton in 1856 - after which they moved to St. Louis, where they resided until the outbreak of war.

Mr. Clayton enlisted, and his wife was determined to accompany him. He procured for his wife, a suit of men's clothes and a false moustache, and they mustered in together into Co. A, 13th MO Cavalry. They both participated in the battle of Stone's River, where he was killed before her eyes and she was badly wounded in a bayonet charge.

CONFUSED
(Three Recruits)

Male disguises were of no effect when two ladies, unused to wearing trousers, reached for their aprons to catch an apple; a third lady reputedly tried to put her trousers on over her head. (44)

MADAME COLLIER
(Two Soldiers)

In his Dec. 23 entry, John Ransom wrote in his Andersonville diary, that a female prisoner named Collier, from East Tennessee, had been found among them, and someone had revealed her sex to the Lieutenant. She having taken a soldier's disguise to be near her lover. Upon being discovered, Madame Collier told of *another female* among them, as yet undiscovered.

SARAH COLLINS
(Soldier - 1st Ky Inf)

A private, [Sarah Collins from Wisconsin] who had served in the First Kentucky Infantry, proved to be of the wrong sex. She performed camp duties with great fortitude, and never fell out of the ranks during the severest marches. She was small in stature, and kept her coat buttoned to her chin. Sarah was from Lake Mills, and had a brother named Mason, who assisted her in enlisting.

She first excited suspicion by her feminine method of putting on her stockings; and when handed over to the surgeon, proved to be a woman about twenty years old. She was discharged from the regiment, but sent to Columbus, OH, upon suspicion (by some of her remarks) that she was a spy of the Rebels. ~~Quoted (18);(22)

ELIZABETH/LIZZIE COMPTON
(Soldier - 125th (?) MI Cav., 11th KY Cav.)

It was reported that Elizabeth served as a trooper with the 125th (?) MI for one year without being discovered. (36) *(Note: Some question as to reports of Elizabeth/Lizzie, being the same person.)*

The *New York Herald,* Dec. 28, 1863, recounts the story of a little girl, who became a soldier. Lizzie was perhaps one of the most tenacious soldier-women of the Civil war. Found wounded and bleeding on the battlefield at Green River Bridge, she was carried to a surgeon's tent. Her sex was discovered during examination when the bindings around her chest were removed to extract the Minie ball from her shoulder.

Upon regaining consciousness hours later, she revealed to the Chaplain that she was sixteen years old and had traveled from her home in London, Canada West, to Virginia at the age of fourteen for the purpose of enlisting in the Union army.

Lizzie recounted how she was discovered after being more seriously wounded at Fredericksburg. Although dismissed from the service at that time, as soon as she recovered, she enlisted again - and again was discovered. Dauntlessly, she persisted and traveled many miles over the mountains to Kentucky where she enlisted again.

In the early years of the war, regulations were lax due to the desperate need for battlefield replacement. Anyone who was willing, and looked like they could fight, was handed a gun. Later, in the last year of the war, soldiers were required to strip to the waist for examination. (6)

When at last Lizzie presented herself at Louisville to be mustered out of 11th Kentucky, she revealed that she had served in no less than seven different regiments, moving from one to another at the prospect of being discovered, and had fought in several battles.

~~~~~~~~~~~~~~~~~~~~~~~~~~~~~

LIZZIE COOK
aka William Ross
(Soldier - 5th KS)

The hospital matron at Benton Barracks, St. Louis, one day had the routine of her official duties varied by detecting the form of a young lady in the habiliments of a young man, the wearer of which was an applicant for enlistment. She was sent to the office of the Department Provost Marshal, where she declined to make any statement as to her name, history, etc.

At length, however, she concluded to tell her story. Her proper name was Lizzie Cook, and her home lay in Aponoose County, Iowa. Her father was in the First Missouri State Militia, and met his death in a skirmish at Walnut Creek, Linn County, MO. Her brother held the position of sergeant in the Fifth Kansas. A desire to reach him, and a disgust at the monotony of woman's life, with a wish to serve her country, led her to determine to assume male attire and volunteer as a soldier.

She accordingly left her home and proceeded to Keokuk, where she worked as a house servant for a family needing such help, till she had earned money enough to buy a suit of boys' clothes. She bought and donned them, and as soon as she had done so, started for St. Louis.

Here she put up at the Everett House, registering her name as Wm. Ross. In the morning she took the cars for Benton Barracks, and was there proposing to enlist, when failing to carry out her disguise to the requisite degree of nicety, she was detected.

Lizzie was a young lady of about twenty summers, tall, fine-looking, intelligent, animated in conversation, and expressed a strong desire to shoulder a musket and do with it what she could for the glorious cause of the Union. It was concluded, however, to commend her to the attention of the Union Aid Society, and greatly to her disappointment, Lizzie was denied the satisfaction of engaging in her country's cause in the way she had marked out.~~Quoted (24)

MARIA COOK (Amiss)
(Mailrider - [W]Va)

When Jones and Imboden raided Burning Springs, Maria Cook delivered mail to them. Maria was the daughter of Paul Cook, who intensely disliked Unionist Bukey. Confederate forces controlled Burning Springs, but Union officials were on the alert to see that no mail reached them from Wood County [W] Virginia.

Miss Maria Cook, as fearless as her father and as strong-willed, her body padded to obesity with letters and mail from close friends and soldiers in the Confederate Army, started from home to deliver her precious cargo to the lines at Burning Springs.

As she rode on horseback, she met the hated Van H. Bukey of Parkersburg. Having been life-long acquaintances, they greeted each other and Bukey asked Maria what she was doing in those parts and where she was going. The wise and shrewd young lady explained her mother was overly tired and she had so much to do she sent Maria to look for a washwoman. She was allowed to continue her journey.

In another incident, Maria rode down Parkersburg's Market Street waving a Confederate flag. When she repeated this later, she was forced to take the loyalty oath, which put an end to the flag waving. ~~Quoted (14)

MARGARETTE COOPER
(Mailrider [W]Va)

Several Confederate women carried mail between Parkersburg [W]VA and the Cooper home at Mineral Wells. Two of the most dedicated were **Maria Cook** (Amiss) and MARGARET COOPER.

Maria and Margaret once took the mail from the Cooper home at Mineral Wells to Parkersburg, and were distributing letters to Confederate families door-to-door. But an informer told Bukey (at the Parkersburg Command Post) and he put a strict curfew on the town. Maria and Margaret were stopped by pickets and sent to the Colonel's headquarters. After crying that they could not get to Maria's home on Core Road, Bukey, a better friend than they realized, personally passed them through the picket line. (See: **Maria COOK** Amiss) ~~Quoted (14)

COPELAND'S DAUGHTERS
(Mailriders)

Two of Colonel Copeland's daughters were arrested for mailrunning in Clarksburg [WV] in the Spring of 1862. ~~Quoted (14)

MARY CORBIN
(Soldier - 89th, 97th OH)

From the Col. Caleb Carleton Papers, 89th OH; Manuscript Div., Library of Congress. Courtesy Tom Sheridan, Regimental Historian.

[When the Army of the Cumberland advanced to the Tennessee River as part of the preliminaries to the Chickamauga Campaign, Carleton and his regiment were left at Tracy City, TN, to guard the rail line that supplied the left wing of the Army.]

Extract from August 27, 1863 letter from Carleton to his wife, Sadie:

"A rather romantic affair in camp today. A person came in dressed in soldier's clothes and claimed to be a private in Wood's Division and wished to go to join a company on our left.

> *But upon being questioned sharply, confessed that she was a woman named Mary Corbin and that she wished to be a soldier, that her father had driven her from home because she kept company with Union soldiers. I hardly know what to do with her as there is nothing but her word to show she is not a spy, but think I will send her to General Rosecrans tomorrow."*

<u>Carleton telegraphed Army HQ about her and got the following response:</u>

> *The General directs that you take every precaution to prevent mischief in case this woman is a spy. -- J.P. Drouillard, Capt. & Aide-de-Camp*

<u>Extract from September 15, 1863 letter, Carleton to Sadie:</u>

> *The female soldier I sent home. She was not a spy. Her story was a hard one. She was rather a fine looking girl, could neither read nor write. A soldier in Wood's Division seduced her upon a promise of marriage. She being romantically disposed, procured a suit of soldier's clothes and intended to follow him. She attracted a good deal of attention and I had to keep a sentinel at her door to keep people out. I sent her out of town at night escorted by the Chaplain and Officer of the Day, and was very glad to get rid of her.*

Mary Corbin was probably from the vicinity of Hillsboro, TN, as it was about that town that Wood's division camped prior to it's advance beyond Tracy City. They camped there from July 7 to August 16. A Sergeant John Wesley Marshall, 97th OH, Wagner's Brigade of Wood's Division wrote an excellent journal of his wartime experience (a transcript of which is in the Ohio Historical Center's Manuscript Collection in Columbus, OH, MSS 679.) His journal entries covering this time make **numerous mention** of the "mountain gazelles" who frequented their camps in great numbers to sell fruits and vegetables to the soldiers.

Also while camped here, the 97th OH, received new uniforms. It is possible that Mary got her "suit of soldier's clothes" from their old, discarded uniforms. Considering that she, in all likelihood, could not return home, and that she was obviously a very enterprising person, it might be that she tried again to join her soldier. Following the defeat at Chickamauga, the army retreated into Chattanooga and remained there for the most part, until the following Spring - so she had the opportunity. (Courtesy: *Tom Sheridan*)

CORPORAL'S BABY
(Soldier - Army of the Potomac)

On April 12, 1863, in a letter home from Falmouth winter camp, Solomon Newton of the 10th Mass, wrote that a baby had been born in camp to a soldier no one had suspected of being a woman, as she'd been in several fights. He added, with a solemn respect,

"... She must have seen some hard times and heard some awful talk, for there was only one knew she was a woman. She must think a good deal of her man, don't you think so? ..."

Naturally, such an event could not escape the attention of the command, therefore:

The following order, as unique in it's way as any that the war gave rise to, can be best explained - if any further explanation be needed - by Major-General Rosecrans:

"Headquarters, Department of the Cumberland, April 17, 1863

"General: - The general commanding directs me to call your attention to a flagrant outrage committed in your command, a person having been admitted inside your lines, without a pass, and in violation of orders. The case is one which calls for your personal attention, and the general commanding directs that you deal with the offending party or parties according to law.

"The medical director reports that an orderly sergeant in Brigadier General_____'s division was today delivered of a baby, - which is in violation of all military law and of the army regulations. No such case has been known since the days of Jupiter. You will apply the proper punishment in this case, and a remedy to prevent a repetition of the act." ~~Quoted (3)

LUCY ANN COX
(Vivandiere - 13th Va)

In a letter dated May 26, 1864, *Henry Besancon,* of the 104th NY, wrote that a woman named Lucy Ann Cox was active as a vivandiere to the 13th Va., however, she later turned her attention to nursing.

CROSSLEY REPORTS
(Trooper - Confederate Cavalry)

In a further exchange of letters between *A. Jackson Crossley* to *S. Bradbury,* Hq., Army of the Potomac, 29 May 1864, it was disclosed that a female cavalry trooper dressed in a Rebel uniform, was arrested as a spy. (See Soldiers' Regiments)

SOPHIA CRYDER
(Soldier - 11th PA, Co.A)

Sophia was an adventurous young lady who enlisted in the Sumner Rifles for pure excitement. Her experience was short-lived, however, when she was recognized by one of her acquaintances from back home, and her disguise exposed after only a week. (See Soldiers' Regiments)

PAULINE CUSHMAN

MAJOR PAULINE CUSHMAN
(Spy)

Beautiful Pauline was born Harriet Wood, in New Orleans, June 10, 1833, the daughter of a merchant from Madrid who anglicized his name, and whose wife was the daughter of a Bordeaux wine grower. She was the only girl, among seven brothers.

At the age of ten, Harriet was named "Laughing Breeze" by the Indians who traded at her father's post in a little frontier town called, Grand Rapids, Michigan.

By the time she was nineteen, Harriet was an actress in New York, and that was when she changed her name to Pauline Cushman. Soon, she became Mrs. Charles Dickinson, and had two children - sadly, both of whom died within a day of each other. Before too much longer, Pauline was a widow when Charles - who served as a musician for the Union - died in 1862.

When the war broke out, Pauline was living in Cleveland, Ohio, and well-known as an actress. Traveling to Louisville for an engagement, she met and became close to certain Rebel officers - even drinking a toast on stage to the Southern cause to gain the South's confidence. This, coupled with the fact that one of her brothers served in a secession regiment in Mississippi, resulted in accusations of her being a secessionist (in spite of her adamant protests), resulted in her arrest.

To put her loyalty to the test, she was asked to join the secret service, and serve as a spy for the Union. Eager to prove her loyalty, she immediately began carrying letters between Louisville and Nashville. Dressed in a Confederate uniform as an aide to Capt. Blackman, she became familiar with the backroads of

Tennessee, N. Georgia, Alabama and Mississippi, and provided invaluable service under Gen. Rosecrans.

She was taken prisoner by the Confederates twice for being a spy, but managed to escape both times. She was not so fortunate, however, during her third capture while scouting the Rebel forces towards Shelbyville. She was captured eleven miles from Shelbyville and two Rebel scouts escorted her toward Forrest's headquarters at Spring Hill. Midway, however, Pauline pretended to be ill and unable to ride any further, so her captors stopped to rest at a house along the way, whereupon they discovered from the resident of the house that a Federal scouting party had passed through not an hour before. Pauline, knowing that her guards carried important papers for General Bragg, conceived a scheme to use to her advantage.

Sensing the compassion held for her from an old negro standing nearby, she placed ten Tennessee dollars in his hand, and asked him to come running and shouting that *"Four hundred Federals are coming down the street !!!"*

Creating much excitement, the old man did as she had asked. Pauline's captors refused to believe until he got down on his knees and begged them to believe him. At last they did, mounted their horses and took off into the woods. Grabbing a pistol from a wounded soldier in the house, Pauline jumped on her mount and took off in the opposite direction.

Riding through the dark and the rain, she lost her way and soon came upon a pickett who challenged her. She pretended to be a friend of Jeff Davis, so the pickett asked her to give the countersign. By presenting a countersign in the shape of a canteen of whiskey, she was able to pass through five picketts, but the sixth and last pickett was not convinced - not even after she pleaded that she was on her way to Franklin to visit a sick uncle.

Discouraged, she turned back and sought shelter from a kindly farmer in a nearby house. He agreed to wake her early in the morning and put her on the right road to Franklin. But the next morning she was awakened to find her horse saddled, and waiting between the two guards from whom she had escaped the night before!

They took Pauline to Forrest's headquarters, and after much questioning, nothing could be found against her, so she was sent to General Bragg. While there, however, a woman stole her gaiters that concealed under the inner sole, important documents that proved she was a spy. Pauline was tried, and sentenced to be executed, but being ill, the sentence was postponed. Finally, after laying in prison for three months, she sent for General Bragg and asked him for mercy. He told her he wanted to make an example of her and would hang her as soon as she was well enough to be hung. Thankfully, before her sentence could be carried out, Rosecran's army captured the town in which she was imprisoned, and she was set free.

Too well known to continue her espionage activities any longer, Pauline returned to the stage before the war had ended. Dressed in a uniform, bearing the rank of Major, she toured the country lecturing on her experiences.

Pauline married August Fichtner in 1877, and then Jerry Fryer in 1879. She had more children, but none lived to be adults. She died on December 2, 1893, at the age of sixty, in San Francisco, California. (23),(24),(28),(34)

MRS. CUSTIS
(Daughter of the Regiment)

Reports of women in military dress were more common among Federal troops than Confederate. Apart from those women who assumed male dress while disguised as soldiers, the vivandiere/daughters assigned to each regiment, either re-fashioned the uniforms of the soldiers with fanciful touches from the ladies' styles of the day - such as Garibaldi jackets, and flowing ostrich plumes in their hats - or created their own original look in "ladies' military fashion".

One very creative daughter was Mrs. Custis of Rochester, New York. She was not very pretty, but caused a great deal of excitement when captured by the Confederates and sent to Richmond. They had never seen anything like her - this lady with military insignias on her hat and chevrons on her sleeves - and could not decide whether to treat her as a civilian or a soldier!

After telling them boldly what she thought of her captors and their cause, they entertained sending her to the military prison. Not seeming to them to be the wisest decision, they settled the problem by renting a private room for her. (23)

FRANCES DAY
aka "Sgt. Frank Mayne"
(Soldier - 126th PA, Co.F)
and
ELVIRA IBECKER
aka "Charles D. Fuller"
(Soldier - 46th PA, Co.D)

In the history of the 126th Regiment of Pennsylvania, it was recorded that both Frances and Elvira enlisted in Pennsylvania regiments and were successful in their disguise as soldiers.

Frances was no different than most of the women who enlisted. She followed her lover, William Fitzpatrick into battle in August of 1862. As Frank Mayne, she had been elected a Sergeant in Co. F. When William died of disease that same month in a Washington camp, however, Frances deserted.

The officers of Co. F were notified later on in the war by the military "out west", that a wounded woman - Frances Day - had been discovered in the ranks. It was later reported that she was killed in battle. (30)

BRIDGET DIVERS

BRIDGET DIVERS
aka Irish Biddy
(Vivandiere - Daughter of the Regiment)
1st Michigan Cavalry

Sometimes called Irish Biddy, sometimes known as Michigan Bridget, this fiery little lady was often the spark that rallied the troops in the foreboding of battle. Wherever she was needed, she was there performing her invaluable services on the field, in the hospitals, and even acting as a surgeon.

There was no skill that she lacked, and no circumstance that could sway or stop her from giving aid to those who needed her. She was brave and fearless under fire and had several horses shot out from under her. She could ride and shoot and often took the place of a fallen comrade in battle.

In an incident at Dinwiddie Court House, where her regiment had been turned back, she boldly rode to the front of the line to retrieve the body of their fallen Captain. The Confederates only stood silently in awe, as they watched her lay his lifeless body over her horse and begin a twelve mile ride to deliver him to the rest of the regiment for burial.

At Fair Oaks, supporting her wounded husband with one arm, she swung her soldier's cap in the air with the other - cheering on the 7th Massachusetts to get revenge for her husband being wounded in the leg. She shouted, *"Arrah! go in, boys, and bate the bloody spalpeens, and revinge me husband, and God be wid ye!"* Whereupon the men gave three rousing cheers for Irish Biddy, and joining with other troops, charged the enemy successfully.

Even after the war, Bridget could not be stopped. She loved life in the cavalry and eventually she crossed the Great Plains with her husband's detachment for Indian service out West. (2),(13),(16),(23),(28)

MRS. ELLIS
(Commander's Wife)
1st Mo. Cav.

Quite a sensation was created in Jefferson City, Missouri one evening by the arrival of Mrs. Colonel Ellis, from Tipton, bearer of dispatches from General Hunter and Colonel Ellis.

She was dressed in a semi-military riding habit and hat, with a crimson sash thrown around the left shoulder as an officer of the day, mounted on a splendid charger, attended by two orderlies.

She had ridden forty-five miles since ten o'clock, and without taking a moments rest, delivered her orders at camp and then waited upon General Price - with her dispatches urging forward two squadrons of Colonel Ellis's command - to join the regiment at Tipton.

This *mulier valiente* was attached to the First Missouri Cavalry as special aid to her husband. ~~Quoted (24)

EMILY
(Soldier - NY)

"Father, forgive your dying daughter. I have but a few moments to live. My native soil drinks my blood. I expected to deliver my country, but the Fates would not have it so. I am content to die. Pray, pa, forgive me. Tell ma to kiss my daguerreotype." -- Emily

Such was a dying girl's last message to her family. Her parents had done everything they could to try to prevent her enlisting - even to sending her to Michigan to stay with an aunt in the hopes she'd give up such a silly notion. She persisted so, that they thought her unbalanced.

Emily was not to be stopped, however, in her determination to become a saviour to the cause. She ran away from her aunt, disguised herself as a drummer, and enlisted in spite of them.

Much to Emily's dismay, however, her mission was short-lived after serving at Tullahoma. On the second day of battle at Chickamauga, she received a wound in the side that proved to be fatal. (30)

ANNA ETHERIDGE

ANNA ETHERIDGE
aka Gentle Annie
(Vivandiere-Daughter of the Regiment)
2nd Mich. Vol.

Anna Blair was born May 3, 1844, in Detroit, Michigan, of Dutch descent. At the time of her birth, her father was a very wealthy man, but while she was still a small child, the family's financial status took a downturn and resulted in their moving to another state (MN/WI?).

When she was twelve, her father died. Only a few short years later, Anna married Mr. Etheridge. In 1861, while visiting in Detroit, Anna enlisted in the Union Army as a vivandiere with the 2nd Michigan Volunteers. Fully equipped and furnished with a horse, Anna prepared to serve to the best of her ability.

By day she drilled and at night slept on the ground alongside the troops. She was a good shot, but the two revolvers she tucked in her belt were reserved for use in the event she was threatened with capture. Her intent was to serve her country on the battlefield as a nurse, and she served it well. Uniformed in a riding habit and military cap, she was a familiar figure on the fields at Bull Run, Antietam, Chancellorsville, Gettysburg, Spottsylvania and many others.

Her saddlebags filled with lint and bandages, and a canteen full of water or "spirits", Anna rode with every charge. As the men fell, she was there to administer to them in any way she could. Once a young soldier from New York was killed by a shell while she was in the act of tending to his wounds. The men so admired and appreciated her that they gave her the name Gentle Annie.

But Anna had a hero's heart. In the volley following her cheering the men on at Chancellorsville, she was wounded in the hand, her horse wounded, and her skirt riddled with bullets. At Spottsylvania she changed the minds of some potential deserters by offering to lead them back into battle.

So brave was Anna that she was awarded the rank of Sergeant Major, but Kearney was killed before he could bestow it upon her. Instead, she was given the Kearney Cross for valor.

In her four years of brave service, some of the time with the 5th Michigan, Anna was responsible for saving hundreds of lives. When she mustered out July 1, 1865, she went to work for the Detroit Treasury. [some conflicting reports say - to support her invalid father]. She worked for the Treasury for thirteen years, after which - for reasons not stated - she was dismissed when she married Mr. Hooks, a soldier who'd lost one of his legs in the war. (2),(23),(28),(30)

SARAH L. EVERSOL
(Heroine)

On the evening of the fifth of February, 1862, at Cape Girardeau, Captain Ben Sousley, in behalf of the Alton Packet Company, presented to the loyal and heroic Mrs. Eversol, the sum of two hundred dollars, in acknowledgment of her courage, humanity and patriotism, in having saved the passengers of the steamboat "City of Alton", from being captured by Jeff. Thompson's marauding band of Confederates.

As that boat was approaching the shore where the secessionists waited to seize her, Mrs. Eversol ran to the levee, and by her shoutings and gesticulations warned those on board of the danger, and enabled them to escape. The handsome testimonial to her merit was richly deserved, but a richer one is assured to her in the memories of her countrymen and countrywomen, for such an unusual, brave, hazardous, and fortunate act.

Captain Sousley subsequently received from Mrs. Eversol the following appropriate note:--

"Commerce, Mo., February 5th
J.J. Mitchell, President Alton Packet Company:

"Dear Sir:

Permit me, through you, to tender to the members of your Company my thanks for the unmerited token of respect which they were pleased to convey to me through the hands of Captain Sousley, and received by me today. In reply to their earnest solicitations to visit St. Louis and Alton, allow me to say that I would be most happy to do so when the weather and traveling are pleasant; although I would again assure them, that, in any part I may have taken on the twenty ninth day of December, in the preservation of the lives of my fellow beings and their property, I only obeyed the impulse of a loyal heart.

With my kindest wishes for the prosperity and happiness of the members of your company and yourself, I remain yours, respectfully,
 -------Sarah L. Eversol"   ~~Quoted (24)

HANNA EWBANK
(Daughter - 7th Wisconsin)

A school-mistress of Marquette...
"In the matter of teaching the young idea how to shoot, Miss Ewbank bore an enviable reputation; but deeming her sphere limited, she has joined the Grand Army, where she may encourage the elder ideas to shoot in a manner peculiarly desirable, and which recommends itself to every patriotic mind.

Her uniform is very neat, consisting of a Zouave jacket of blue merino, trimmed with military buttons and gold lace; a skirt of scarlet merino, trimmed with blue and gold lace; pants and vest of white Marseilles; balmoral boots; hat of blue velvet trimmed with white and gold lace, with yellow plumes, and white kid gloves.

A more jaunty or bewitching little Daughter of the Regiment never handled the canteen, and it is no wonder that the multiplex father jealously watches her, and has sworn sacredly to defend her." ~~Quoted from source. (courtesy: *Eleanor Hoffman*)

FAMILY RESEMBLANCE
(66th IN)

A Kentucky newspaper reported that a young woman in uniform was recognized by her uncle and subsequently sent home. From a prominent family, no names were publicly released. The young lady was quite distraught at being dismissed and wore her uniform home. (44)

AMANDA COLBURN FARNHAM
(Soldier)

Of the many women who served as soldiers during the Civil War, unfortunately few names have been recorded. One who is remembered is Amanda Colburn Farnham, from St. Johnsbury, Vermont.

Amanda, and no doubt in the company of others whose names have been lost, marched through the knee-deep mud to fight in the Seven Day's battles. (23)

FIFTY-NINTH OHIO
(Two Soldiers)

Susan B. Anthony reported in 1881 that two women served as soldiers for three years in the 59th Ohio. (36)

ELIZABETH CAIN FINNAN
(Soldier-Vivandiere)

Noted in the *National Tribune*, Wash., D.C., July 25, 1907, was a report from a Greensburg correspondent from the *Indianapolis News* relative to an obituary that appeared for Elizabeth Cain Finnan, a vivandiere and part-time soldier woman in male attire who took part in some battles. (See Soldiers' Regiments)

ANTONIA FORD
(Lieutenant, C.S.A.)

Also noted in the *National Tribune* on February 25, and March 3, 1932 was a request for recognition of services to the South for Antonia Ford. Antonia served as a Lieutenant in the Confederate army, having been commissioned by General J.E.B. Stuart.

FORTY-NINTH GEORGIA
(Two Soldiers)

From Camp Neal on March 6, 1864, *Sgt. Major Fitzpatrick* mentions in a letter home to his family that two women discovered in uniform with the 49th Georgia were refused permission to cross the Shenandoah River with General Thomas and his troops.

AUGUSTA FOSTER
(Soldier)

Kady Brownell and Anna Etheridge were not the only women in the battle of Bull Run. Although we can never know just how many there were, we do know that Augusta, a soldier from Maine, was there. During the battle, Augusta had her horse shot from under her, but was able to make good her escape. Safely reaching Alexandria, Augusta turned her efforts to tending the sick and wounded. (23)

FOURTEENTH IOWA
(Soldier)

It was reported that a soldier, discovered to be female, chose death over discovery and took her own life.

FREEMANTLE's REPORT
(Soldier)

In Freemantle's report of 1864, he mentions having met a female soldier in disguise who fought in the battles of Perryville and Murfreesboro. Curious to hear the opinions of her comrades, he was told they didn't mind her being there as long as she didn't cause any trouble.

MAJOR G_____

On lighter note, there is the story of the anonymous Mrs. G_____, wife of a slain officer, who was promoted by the President of the United States to the position of Major in the army, in recognition of her bravery in the field and services in the hospital to the Union soldiers. The female Major afterwards sojourned in Cleveland for some days, and finally was married there to a private in the Forty-ninth New York regiment - a mere boy.

The happy couple subsequently visited an artist's studio for the purpose of having their likenesses taken. The lady Major, after inquiring the price of several cases - and failing to be suited thereat - exclaimed, "If you knew who I am, perhaps you would give me a picture!" She then exhibited to the operator several badges, etc., and made known her name and position.

"I can see no reason why you should not pay for a picture, and a good round price at that, for you are getting a pretty plump salary ," said mister operator. "That may be," archly replied the bright woman, "but do you see that 'ere boy?" pointing to her husband: "In all probability, besides having him to take care of, I shall have his dad and mammy on my hands soon!"

Matters were finally "adjusted," and Mrs. Major G___ did not leave without a picture of herself and "boy". ~~Quoted (24)

MARY GALLOWAY
(Soldier - Union Army)

Clara Barton, during a lecture around 1866, told the story of Mary Galloway, a soldier wounded at Antietam, whom she took care of at the Poffenberger farm.

Clara discovered that the soldier was a woman who'd enlisted to be near her husband. After the war, Mr. and Mrs. Galloway named their first child after Clara.

ELLA HOBART GIBSON
(Chaplain - 1st Wisconsin Artillery)

Military records in the National Archives reveal that Mrs. Gibson was probably the only woman to have officially served in the position of Chaplain.

In 1864, she was elected Chaplain of the 1st Wisconsin Artillery and served for nearly a year. After the war, she lectured in the North, but was reluctant to discuss her war experiences. (22)

ELLEN GOODRIDGE
(Soldier)

One of the most touching stories of ill-fated lovers is that of Ellen and her Lieutenant lover, James Hendrick.

After serving for three months in 1861, the Lieutenant received his commission and notified Ellen and his parents that he'd enlisted for three years. Not able to bear being separated, Ellen prepared to join him - against the protests of her parents. Their disappointment with their daughter's wisdom, led her parents to disown her.

Ellen and James fought side by side through the great encounters in Virginia, where Ellen was wounded by a minie ball in the arm. For four years they served in the thickest of battle together until James became very ill.

When he was sent to a Washington hospital, she never left his side, but James grew worse despite her loving care. Their last few days together had begun. An Episcopal clergyman was called to join them together as man and wife - this brave soldier and his soon-to-be young widow who had given all to follow him, but who would received in return, only his name in death. (15)

VICTORIA E. GOODWIN

<u>Found in the deserted office of *THE APPEAL*, 1862,</u>

"A CHALLENGE"

"Where as the wicked policy of the president - making war upon the south for refusing to submit to wrong too palpable for Southerners to do. And where as it has become necessary for the young men of our country, my brother, in the number to enlist to do the dirty work of driving the mercenarys from our sunny south. Whose soil is too holy for such wretches to tramp And whose atmosphere is to pure for them to breathe "For such an indignity afford to civilization I merely challenge any abolition or black republican lady of character if there can be such a one found among the negro equality tribe. To meet me at Masons and dixon line. With a pair of Colt's repeaters or any other weapon they may choose that I may receive satisfaction for the insult." -- Spring Dale, Miss., April 27, 1861 ~~Quoted (18)

GRANT'S AUNT
(Mailrider)

Confederate mail transportation north of Wood County [West] Virginia was dangerous and not well organized. The penalty could be death.

General Ulysses S. Grant's aunt lived about fifty miles east of Charleston, on the road to Kanawah Falls. An intense Confederate, she often carried the mail, and probably was a link in the service from Wood County, Arnoldsburg, the Great Kanawah Valley, and on to Greenbrier County. ~~Quoted (14)

MARY JANE GREEN
(Guerrilla - C.S.A.)

Mary Jane Green was probably the most dedicated, unforgiving, brave, and cantankerous Confederate lady guerrilla in the Little Kanawah Valley during the Civil War. Telegraph wire cutting was her specialty, from Wood County to Clarksburg [WV].

In August 1861, she was arrested for spying and moved to Atheneum Prison in Wheeling. Her disruptiveness in prison far outweighed her threat to Union communications. She was released, but on her way to Grafton, the sight of the hated telegraph lines was too tempting. She left the train and resumed interrupting the army's communication system. She was again arrested and sent to Atheneum Prison, bound in ropes from head to foot, and deposited in a cell.

One of the prison officials tried to calm the fears of what he thought was an ignorant mountain girl in a strange environment. When he thought he had quieted her, he cut her bonds. She promptly hit him in the chest with a brick and broke some of his ribs.

Mary Jane was placed on parole in a private home in Wheeling, but continued unmitigated hell-raising. Dressed in men's clothing, she freely wandered about the military establishment on Wheeling Island with kindred spirits. No further record of Mary Jane Green has been found. ~~Quoted (14)

ELSA JANE/CHARLOTTE GUERIN
aka Charles Hatfield/"Mountain Charley"
(Lieutenant - 4th Iowa Cavalry)

One of the most interesting turnabouts in the life of a woman who fought disguised as a man, is that which happened to Elsa Guerin. Before the war, colorful Elsa was a sailor on the Mississippi and a "mule whacker" on a wagon train to Kansas. But in 1862, she enlisted in the Iowa Cavalry and as *Charles Hatfield*, earned the rank of Lieutenant. She served as an orderly, and later volunteered as a spy. In 1864, as a spy, she successfully managed to steal some important papers. A few days later, however, she was seriously wounded in a cavalry charge which resulted in her being taken prisoner and later exchanged for Confederate wounded.

Elsa was convinced that her military career was over, due to the fact that her sex had been discovered by both the Confederate and Union doctors who had tended her wounds. But, to her amazement, she found that not only had neither doctor divulged her secret, but also that she had even been promoted to 1st Lieutenant under General Curtis! Elsa mustered out in 1865, and was known to have been in male attire for thirteen years.(37)

Much confusion surrounds this soldier's story. So much so, that it is possible that there were two different Mountain Charleys. If this is the case, then fact and legend have no doubt entwined themselves into one story and will be difficult to untangle with so little documentation available. (44)

"CHARLEY H_____"
(Soldier)

Dr. J. A. Edison, of the 148th Illinois, reported on August 12, 1882, that he had knowledge of a girl soldier who died in the U.S. General Hospital, Tullahoma, TN, in the Spring of 1865.
(USAMHI Ref. #57)

NANCY HART

NANCY HART, C.S.A.
(Guerrilla - Moccasin Rangers)

The Moccasin Rangers in Calhoun Co. [WV.] began as home guards, but later became a guerrilla band. Perry Connolly was the acknowledged leader of the outlaw Moccasin Rangers. He was the most cruel and bloodthirsty of all the guerrilla Captains and was most feared by the people of Wood County. Company A, 11th WV. Infantry called themselves the "Snake Hunters" as they made life miserable for the Moccasins.

Nancy Hart was Perry Connolly's girlfriend and the only ordained full-time woman member of the Moccasin Rangers. Many Union soldiers learned to their sorrow that Nancy was a determined, fearless woman, as deadly as a copperhead snake. She rode at the head of the column with Perry and together they made the rules and enforced them.

Trapped along the West Fork River, Perry escaped and Nancy was captured. Arrested, Nancy turned on her flowers-in-May country innocence, was judged not to be a threat to the Union, and was released. She returned immediately to the Rangers and warned Connolly that his life was in danger. Perry Connolly, scourge of the Baltimore and Ohio Railroad from Parkersburg to Clarksburg was, however, about to meet his doom.

On Jan 2, 1862, the Moccasin Rangers were caught with their backs to their enemies in a complete state of unreadiness, at Welch Glade. Captain Connolly was badly injured and unable to run. But he fought the Union soldiers like a cornered animal, and was finally beaten to death by gunbutts.

After Capt. Connolly's death, [with a large price on her head] Nancy was captured [in July 1862 by Lt. Col. Starr, 9th [WV] and held in Summersville, but managed to escape by winning the confidence of one of her Union Guards so far as to secure his musket. No sooner had she grasped the musket in her hands, however, than she stepped back in the room, and lifting it to her shoulder, fired. Her guard fell dead at his post. Nancy, jumping over his body, rushed downstairs and out to the barn, where she mounted Colonel Starr's horse, and without saddle or bridle, fled away before the sleeping officials could possibly realize what had happened... a week later, she appeared at the head of a battalion of Jackson's cavalry, five hundred strong, under the command of Major Bailey, "who surrounded our headquarters and captured us without much resistance."

Nancy transferred her loyalty to Capt. Geo. Downs' company of Moccasin Rangers and became romantically attached to Joshua Douglas, a member of Downs' company. Nancy and Joshua later moved to Greenbrier County, where they lived for many years. ~~Quoted (14)

MARGARET HENRY
and
MARY WRIGHT, C.S.A.

Throughout the war, newspapers carried reports of countless women disguised in uniform. These two Southern ladies, described as "dashing young creatures", wound up in prison in Nashville. They were captured only two weeks before the end of the war. (22)

ELLA HERBERT
(Mailrider)

It is difficult to perceive the obstacles many daring young women overcame in their participation in war activities. Those who carried the mail to troops spent many long, hard hours in the saddle. Ella was a local heroine - earning her fame carrying mail from Missouri to Southern troops in Mississippi. Her exploits may never have won her a medal, but they did win her a husband. (22)

MARY HILL
(Vivandiere)

This `semi-soldier' followed her brother to war and served the troops as a vivandiere. Unlike some female camp followers, Mary conducted herself in such a way that she was highly respected by all who knew her. (27)

JENNIE HODGERS

JENNIE/GEORGIE HODGERS
aka Albert Cashier
(Soldier - 95th Ill.,Co.G)

Jennie was born in Ireland, but as a youngster, she came to the United States as a stowaway (no doubt disguising herself as a boy). She first lived in the midwest and dressing in male attire, worked as a shepherd and farmer.

When she was nineteen, she enlisted in the Army and served successfully as "Albert D. Cashier" for three years - August 1862-1865. The war record of Albert is impressive, having served in the Red River Campaign, at Nashville, Vicksburg, Gunntown, and in the Meridian Campaign. Albert was known by his comrades to be very small (five feet), somewhat reclusive and hard to get to know - but a good soldier.

Jenny's career ended with the capture of Mobile, and her assumed name has been forever etched into history with over 36,000 other soldiers whose names appear on the Vicksburg Monument. Even after Jennie returned to civilian life, she maintained her masculine disguise, and drew a pension in 1899.

In 1911, however, Jennie's secret was exposed when she was hospitalized after being hit by the Governor's car. When her story made the papers, she was visited by some of her fellow soldiers who expressed their surprise to learn that "Albert" was a woman. In a sworn testimony given to the Bureau of Pensions in 1914, one of her former comrades testified that none of them suspected her true gender, as no physical examinations were required. He had enlisted with "Albert", on the same day and only had to show their hands.

After her injury, she remained in the Soldiers' and Sailors' Home in Quincy, IL until her death at age 71 in October of 1915. She was buried with full military honors in Saunemin Cemetery, Watertown, IL, and her tombstone bears the name of "Albert D. Cashier". (1),(13) (Also, Washington Sunday Star, Mar 29, 1913; Nat'l Tribune, 21 Aug 1913; Nat'l Tribune 23 Aug 1923; and Nat'l Archives Pension File # C2,573,248.

ANNA HOLSTEIN
(Battlefield Nurse at Antietam)

Anna was born in Muncy, PA, on April 9, 1824, the daughter of Rebecca and William Ellis. She was married to Maj. Wm. H. Holstein in 1848 and they resided on a farm in Montgomery Co., PA, until the war began.

For awhile, after Maj. Holstein went off to battle, Anna worked in her hometown Soldier's Aid Society doing whatever she could to help. Some of her neighbors tried to convince her to take up nursing, but Anna shrank from the possibility.

Soon, however, her husband returned to tell her of the sufferings of the battlefield and convinced her of how desperately her services were needed. Anna and William gave up their home to follow the troops from battle to battle for three years, regardless of the dangers.

In 1867 Anna wrote a book anonymously about her experiences, entitled "Three Years in Field Hospitals of the Army of the Potomac", and went on to continue her service through the Valley Forge Centennial and Memorial Association. She died in Bridgeport, PA, Dec. 13, 1900. (7 p.210-11);(23 p. 373) Also see Biddle's, "Notable Women of PA". U of PA Press, 1942.

FRANCES HOOK

FRANCES HOOK
aka Frank Miller/Henderson
(Soldier - 19th, 90th IL Inf., 65th IL Home Guards)

Frances Hook's parents died when she was only three years old, and left her with a brother in Chicago, Illinois. Soon after the war commenced, she and her brother enlisted in the 65th Home Guards. Frances assumed the name of "Frank Miller." She served three months and was mustered out without the slightest suspicion of her sex having arisen.

She then enlisted in the 19th Ill., to be near her brother and participated in its engagements. She next enlisted in the 3rd Ill., and served for several months, during which time she managed to retain her secret, and by her staid habits won the universal esteem of the officers.

Wounded in one of the battles in which she participated, she was discharged. But "Frank's" love for the service did not permit her long to pursue the inert life incident to home, and the organization of the 19th Ill. regiment offered her an opportunity to gratify her love for a military life.

She served in all the battles of that regiment, and was present at the capture of Holly Springs by the rebels. The capture was denounced by her as a disgraceful proceeding on the part of our forces, whom she felt could have held the place.

She was taken prisoner in a battle near Chattanooga. While attempting to escape she was shot through the calf. The rebels searched her person for papers and discovered her sex. The rascals respected her person as a woman, and gave her a separate room while in prison at Atlanta, Ga.

During her captivity she received a letter from Jeff. Davis, offering her a Lieutenant's commission if she would enlist in their army. She had no home and no relatives, but she said she preferred to fight as a private soldier for the stars and stripes rather than be honored with a commission from the "rebs."

While the army was at Chattanooga, Colonel [Joseph W]. Burke, of the 10th OH, went out to Graysville, Georgia, under flag of truce, with authority from General Thomas to exchange twenty-seven prisoners in our hands for an equal number in the hands of the rebels, the preliminaries of which had been previously arranged. Among the number in the hands of the enemy was a member of the 19th Illinois, who may be called "Frank Henderson".

At last she was exchanged. [They] tried to extort from her a promise that she would go home, and not enter the service again. "Go home;" she said, "my only brother was killed at Pittsburgh Landing, and I have no home - no friends!" She then enlisted in [Col. Timothy O'Meara's] 90th IL, Co. G.

In the latter part of the summer of 1863, while the regiment was marching through Florence, Alabama, she asked and obtained permission of her Colonel to enter a house in search of something to eat; her regiment moved on, and while waiting for the supper to be prepared in the house where she was, two rebels crawled out from under a bed, and presenting themselves before her, ordered her to surrender.

Thus in their power, she was forced to yield herself a prisoner, and was taken to Atlanta, and there placed in duress. In a few weeks after her arrival, "Frank" made a desperate attempt to escape, and when ordered to halt by the guard, paid not the least attention to the demand, and was fired upon. The ball took effect in her leg, and she continued to suffer from the wound.

Colonel Burke, while out with the flag of truce, effected her exchange, among others, and she became an inmate of the hospital, where in due time she happily recovered from her wounds. From the time of her first enlistment, which was in June 1861, until some weeks after her capture, she kept her sex a secret from everybody, nor was there ever any suspicion excited in regard to her not being of the sex whose attire she wore.

In personal appearance she was prepossessing, and her whole demeanor was such as would have done no discredit to the best man in the ranks. "Frank" is described as of about medium height, with dark hazel eyes, dark brown hair, rounded features, and feminine voice and appearance. ~~~Quoted (24 p. 172;567)

National Tribune - Aug. 29, 1895
<u>Letter to the Editor from Nat. Mullin, 10th IL, Co.H</u>

"...I was captured Dec, 18, 1863, and at once sent to Atlanta, Ga., where I found several of our wounded prisoners from the field of Chickamauga, and among the number, a girl of medium stature by the alias of Frank Miller, Co. G., 90th Ill.

... I omitted to state that during my stay at Atlanta there was a special exchange, and among the number who were included was the girl referred to [as] Frank___Miller ... She wore a complete Yankee uniform suit." (USAMHI Ref. #1674)

NOTE: The account "**WOUNDED AT CHICKAMAUGA**" may also relate to the above, Frances Hook. Also see "**FRANK MARTIN**" and "**THREE WHO DIED**". (Frances may also have served in the 2nd E. TN Cav., and the 8th MI)

LUCINDA HORNE
(Vivandiere - Co.K, 14th SC Vol)

Lucinda was recruited as a vivandiere and left their home in a German settlement of Edgefield County to follow her husband and son into war. She tended as well, to the many needs of the other men in their regiment. She was so well liked and appreciated that they made her an honorary member.(27) (Also see Chapman's "History of Edgefield Co.", p. 483, 489-91.)

KATE W. HOWE
aka Tom Smith
(Soldier)

During 1885, the *National Tribune* carried several accounts regarding the granddaughter of Gen. Winfield Scott, who claimed to have enlisted in the Union Army under the name of Tom Smith, as a drummer boy.

She was in the battle of Lookout Mountain where she was wounded and her sex then discovered. She drew a soldier's pension of $17 a month. (USAMHI Ref. # 4729 - Nat'l Tribune, 10 Sep, 29 Oct, 26 Nov, 10 Dec 1885)

EMMA HUNT
(Soldier - IN Cav?)

A notation on back of a photo of two soldiers which appeared in the May / Jun 1991, issue of Military Images, reads ... "Emma Hunt and her Uncle, Rockport Parke City, Ind." Both are in uniform."

MRS. HUNTER
(Saboteur)

Mrs. Hunter confessed, along with her daughter, to deliberately destroying several bridges in Tennessee. Their mission was to block Federal advances. The fearless and effective Southern women boldly added that they'd readily do it again if they ever got the chance. Rosecrans wanted to make sure they didn't get another chance and sent them back to Confederate lines. (22)

"CHARLES JOHEHOUS"
(Soldier-6th MO Inf.)

"In disinterring the Federal dead near Resaca, Ga., a body was discovered which excited considerable attention from the smallness of the feet. On examination it was found to be that of a woman shot through the head. The grave was marked, `Charles Johehous, Private, 6th Mo.'"

Nat'l Tribune, Wash. D.C., 13 May 1886 - P.D. Davis

"JOHNNY"

"Johnny was apparently about 17 years old, slight in form, clear, fair complexion, brown eyed and attractive. Who he really was we never knew. We first saw him while on the march to Green River, Ky; it was afternoon, and very hot when he quietly fell in by the side of an orderly of one of the companies, and after a short conversation said in a pleasant voice, "You look so tired. Let me carry your knapsack; it will rest you." The Sergeant, being glad to get rid of his load, gave him the knapsack as requested. He knew that the boy, who said his name was Johnny, did not belong to our regiment, and could only learn that he was a citizen, and that his home was in Pennsylvania.

Towards night we came to a body of timber through which a creek ran; here we halted to camp, and when the boys broke ranks, Johnny was in his element, full of fun, throwing sticks in the water to spatter the boys who were trying to wash the dust from their heated faces, singing snatches of songs, and making merry generally.

Soon the fires were blazing all about the camp. The smell of fried bacon and the aroma of coffee was rapidly sharpening our appetites. The Sergeant and Lieutenant of his company were patiently waiting the slow movements of their cook, a dilapidated old darkey, when Johnny, taking in the situation, asked permission to help get supper. Without an answer (a look from the Lieutenant being sufficient), he rolled up his sleeves, washed his hands and arms, and in a short time had some splendid light biscuits baked, the bacon was fried to a nice brown, some eggs was cooked and temptingly placed on the bright tin plates, washed and brightened while supper was cooking. For weeks after, Johnny cooked for this mess and always had everything neat and tidy.

In a few days we arrived at our destination. By this time the whole detachment had become acquainted with Johnny, and all liked him. Yet the sly glances cast at him, and the whispered conversations carried on in the groups here and there, showed that the boys suspicioned him of something. At last it came out; Johnny was believed to be a girl, and on being taken to headquarters and questioned, admitted, with tears streaming down her cheeks, that she was, and begged that she might be allowed to stay with us.

A fight with the enemy was liable to occur at any hour, and no time was to be had now to send her out of the lines. The next morning, at daybreak, the expected battle began and raged furiously for three hours. During all this time Johnny was on every portion of the field, reckless of danger, between the contending lines, giving the wounded water or such attention as they most needed, tenderly caring for all, Union and Rebel alike. When the battle ceased her clothing and bare arms were red with blood. Seeing the Colonel just then, she touched her cap and said: "*Didn't we whip them nicely. Three cheers for our brave Colonel.*" The next day the command started to join its brigade and when we reached Lebanon, Johnny was left behind.

Months passed. Sherman's victorious army of which our regiment was a part, had surrounded Atlanta; fighting was constant and furious and one of our men, among many others, was badly wounded and conveyed to a hospital at Marietta. While there, half delirious with pain, he was awakened by a hand laid gently in his and a woman's voice saying, "*Don't you know me? I am Johnny.*"

At first he did not recognize her, as she was now dressed in women's apparel. But when he looked again, he knew she indeed was Johnny, and to that poor boy, sick in body and in mind from the loss of limb, it was like meeting a long-lost sister. It is needless to say that from thence on until he was able to go home, he had every care that it was possible to give. Johnny was with him nearly every hour, as tenderly nursing him as a mother. They had many conversations regarding her life, but he could never learn anything definite about her.

She was one of those mysteries of which army life was full. Perhaps some great wrong, some great sorrow drove her from home. Of this we may never know; but we do know that many a brave boy who was wounded or sick, will never forget Johnny".
~Quoted (USAMHI Ref. # 193 - Nat'l Tribune, 25 Sep 1884)

MARY JANE JOHNSON
(Soldier - 11th KY Cav.)

"This morning, a young woman was discovered in camp on Belle Island, belonging to the 11th KY Cavalry, named Mary Jane Johnson, sixteen years of age. She has been in the Union Army a year; has neither father nor mother, and was induced to join the army by the Captain of her company, who was killed in the battle where she was taken prisoner. She was sent over to Richmond to be sent North."

Belle Island Prison - 9 Dec 1863, *Journal entry of W.W. Sprague, 13th Mass., Co. B* ~Quoted (USAMHI Ref. #652).

ANNIE JONES
(Vivandiere - NY Rgt)

It is believed that Annie first joined the ranks as a vivandiere sometime after the regiment reached Washington, although some of the officers insisted she'd been with them prior to that. (22)

LIZZIE JONES
(Regimental Daughter - 6th Mass. Vol.)

From the time of her first appearance in camp, she proved a great comfort to the soldiers in the hospital, visiting them daily, and dispensing among the unfortunate many a little delicacy, as well as going frequently through the streets of the camp with strawberries, cherries, etc. Sometimes she distributed as many as sixteen boxes to a company - the market-man, of course, driving his cart to each tent.

And now the men were honoring her services by presenting her with a very special gift. The presentation speech accompanying the gift of a new and beautiful uniform, was made by Sergeant Crowley, of Lowell. She was given a gold lace trimmed jacket of dark velvet; and a red, white and blue silk skirt. The new hat was light-colored, and decorated with red, white and blue feathers. On the side of the hat was a gold emblem consisting of a wreath encircling the number "6". Her uniform was completed with a beautiful, embossed silver canteen.

She took the box containing the uniform, and with the canteen over her shoulder, tripped lightly into the `hospital' that was close at hand, and in a few moments re-appeared in her new and beautiful attire. Standing upon the green, with the beautiful silk banners on each side, she addressed the regiments as follows: --

"Comrades - when you took me, a stranger, and adopted me as your daughter, I had but little idea of what you were doing, and what my duties were; but having been in camp with you two months, and learned to know you all, I have learned to love you all, and I feel that you all love me, because there are none of you when we meet but have a kind word and a pleasant smile for me. And now that you have put me in uniform, I feel still more that I belong to you, and I will try never to forget it. But you do not expect me to talk, but, like this splendid treasure [canteen], which I shall prize as a remembrance to the last day of my life - which is full to relieve the parched lips of my sick and wounded comrades - so shall my heart be a canteen full of love and sympathy for each and all of you. Comrades, thank you, thank you, thank you."

The little daughter delivered the speech in a very clear and distinct manner, and at its conclusion the regiment gave her three cheers and a "tiger," and escorted her to headquarters. (20) (24)

·**Lizzie Jones was only ten years old.**

NELLIE A. K_____
(Soldier - 102nd NY)

Nellie and her brother were from Long Island, and together they enlisted and fought at Antietam, Chancellorsville, Gettysburg and Lookout Mountain. When her sex became known, however, she was sent home and her brother refused to allow her to re-enlist.

She begged the famous spy, Pauline Cushman to help her re-enlist, and told her that she laid awake at night desiring to be in the fight and "cursing the fate" that made her a girl. (22)

~~~~~~

MRS. ABREV KAMOO
aka "Tommy Kamoo"
(Soldier)

It is an unfortunate fact that women's participation in the Battle of Gettysburg, as well as the Civil War, has mostly been overlooked. Too often, stories involving women in the ranks are not documented well enough to positively identify either the person or her actions.

The following is such a case:

In 1904, a Lancaster, Pennsylvania newspaper reported that Mrs. Abrev Kamoo had recently died in a Boston hospital. According to the article, Kamoo had been born in Tunis in 1815, and had later attended the University of Heidelberg. In 1862 (age 47) she had come to the U.S. where she disguised herself as "Tommy" Kamoo and immediately joined the Union Army.

During the war she served as a nurse and drummer, her sex being kept hidden all the while. Mrs. Kamoo said she took part in the Battle of Gettysburg where she was slightly wounded in the nose. ~~Quoted (10)

KATE
(Soldier - 116th Ill.)

Many a soldier's letters home contained accounts of women discovered in the ranks...

"The Colonel gives our 1st Lt. fits today after drill about Kate. She goes in men's clothes. She has been with the Regiment ever since we left Memphis .... you could hardly tell her from a man." (41)

KILLED AT ANTIETAM
(Soldier)

In her memoirs, Sarah Seeleye tells of burying this unidentified female soldier with her own hands...

"In passing among the wounded after they had been carried from the field, my attention was attracted to the pale, sweet face of a youthful (blonde) soldier who was severely wounded in the neck. The wound still bled profusely, and the boy was growing faint from loss of blood. I stooped down and asked him if there was anything he would like to have done for him. The soldier turned a pair of beautiful, clear, intelligent eyes upon me for a moment in an earnest gaze, and then as if satisfied with the scrutiny, said faintly:

"Yes, yes; there is something to be done, and that quickly, for I am dying ... I can trust you, and will tell you a secret. I am not what I seem, but am a female.

I enlisted from the purest motives, and have remained undiscovered and unsuspected. I have neither father, mother nor sister. My only brother was killed today. I closed his eyes about an hour before I was wounded. I shall soon be with him.

I am a Christian, and have maintained the Christian character ever since I entered the army. I have performed the duties of a soldier faithfully, and am willing to die for the cause of truth and freedom. My trust is in God, and I die in peace. I wish you to bury me with your own hands, that none may know after my death that I am other than my appearance indicates. I know I can trust you - you will do as I have requested?"

Sarah buried her on the battlefield under a mulberry tree.

KILLED AT PICKETT'S CHARGE
(Soldier)

The Official Records contain a report made by General Hays regarding the Gettysburg burials, that a Confederate woman and her husband had been killed during the Pettigrew-Trimble-Pickett charge and were buried by Hay's men on July 3rd. (10)

(See: Pickett's Division)

KILLED AT SHILOH
(Soldier)

In 1934, Mr. Mancil Milligan uncovered human bones while putting in a garden at his home, located just outside the Shiloh Battlefield Park. Investigators found it to be the burial site of nine Union soldiers who died at the battle of Shiloh. Further investigation revealed, however, that one of the soldiers was a woman - killed by a minie ball. (13)

JOSIE KING
(Heroine)

When her father, the Reverend Mr. T.S.N. King of Pine Bluff, Arkansas, was brutally murdered by stragglers, the men who did it were pursued by his daughter, Josie, for a distance of thirty miles. She then reported the outrage to General Steele, who had the men arrested and punished for their crime. ~~ Quoted (17)

LADY AT BLUE LICKS
(Soldier - Ky Rgt)

At the time when the Federal troops were quartered at Blue Licks, Ky, the monotony of camp life was broken by a rather romantic incident. Several recruits were coming in daily, and were immediately sworn into service, but one spruce little fellow arriving Sunday evening, refused to take the oath on the Lord's day, wishing to postpone it until next morning, which modest request was granted.

The young recruit sauntered leisurely around among the men, apparently perfectly at home. When the time came to "turn in", he was shown a bed with three or four soldiers in the same room, which he readily accepted. His fellow-lodgers attempted to converse, but found him quite silent, and, observing him kneel for prayer before retiring, they concluded he was too pious for a soldier, but was perhaps to be chaplain.

Next morning the surgeon was sent to have a conversation with the recruit before the oath was administered, and he being rather observing than otherwise, concluded, after a short "confab," that the young soldier was a very pretty female. After considerable blushing, she acknowledged the fact, stating that her intended was in the ranks, and that she was determined to accompany him.

It seems that "cruel parents," as usual, were the cause, they having refused to let the young folks marry, and, in the desperation of the moment, the young swain sought the army, and a night or two following, the lovestricken maiden donned a suit of her brother's clothes, and joined her lover at Camp Blue Lick.

The Colonel discharged the young Romeo the next morning, and that evening the fortunates were made one.~~ Quoted (24)

ANNIE LILLYBRIDGE
(Soldier - 21st MI)

Annie Lillybridge of Detroit, was for "Union," and in favor of the hardships and dangers of war, if need be, to secure that end. She courted, rather than shrank from, those hardships, and bared her breast to rebel bullets.

According to Annie's account, her parents resided in Hamilton, Canada West. In the spring of 1862, she was employed in a dry goods store in Detroit, where she became acquainted with Lieutenant W--, of one of the Michigan regiments, and an intimacy immediately sprang up between them. They corresponded for some time, and became much attached to each other. But during the ensuing summer season, Lieutenant W-- was appointed to a position in the twenty-first Michigan infantry, then rendezvousing in Ionia county.

The thought of parting from the gay Lieutenant nearly drove Annie mad, and she resolved to share his dangers and be near him. No sooner had she resolved upon this course than she proceeded to act. Purchasing male attire she visited Ionia, and enlisted in Captain Kavanaugh's company, twenty-first regiment. While in camp she managed to keep her secret from all; not even the object of her attachment, who met her every day, was aware of her presence so near him.

Annie left with her regiment for Kentucky, passed through all the dangers and temptations of a camp-life, endured long marches, and slept on the cold ground - all without a murmur. At last, before the battle of Pea Ridge, in which her regiment took part, her sex was curiously discovered by a member of her company, upon whom she laid the injunction of secrecy, after relating to him her previous history.

On the following day she was under fire, and from a letter in her possession, it appears she behaved with marked gallantry, and by her own hand shot a rebel Captain who was in the act of firing upon Lieutenant W--. But the fear of revealing her sex continually haunted her.

After the battle, she was sent out with others, to collect the wounded, and one of the first corpses found by her was the soldier who had discovered her sex. Days and weeks passed on, and she became a universal favorite with the regiment; so much so, that her colonel, [Ambrose A. Stevens, 21st MI], frequently detailed her as regimental clerk - a position that brought her in close contact with her lover, who at this time, was Major or Adjutant of the regiment.

A few weeks subsequently she was out on picket duty, when she received a shot in the arm that disabled her, and notwithstanding the efforts of the surgeon, her wound grew worse from day to day. She was sent to the hospital at Louisville, where she remained several months, then she was discharged by the post surgeon, as her arm was stiffened and useless.

Annie implored to be permitted to return to her regiment, but the surgeon was unyielding, and discharged her. Annie immediately hurried toward home. At Cincinnati she told her secret to a benevolent lady, and was supplied with female attire. She declared she would enlist in her old regiment again, if there was a recruiting officer for the twenty-first in Michigan. She still clung to the Lieutenant - said she must be near him if he fell, or was taken down sick - that where he went she would go - and when he died, she would end her life by her own hands. ~Quoted (3 p. 442-43);(24 p. 621)

[NOTE: The only two officers whose last names begin with "W", serving in the 21st MI Inf., were Lt. Col. Morris B. Wells (p. 159) and Lt. Col. Wm. L. Whipple (p. 160) - Ref: Historical Register and Dictionary of the U.S. Army, Vol. II, Gov't. Printing Office, Wash., 1903.]

MADEMOISELLE MAJOR
(Officer, C.S.A)

A Union soldier named Bently, related the following experience regarding his capture by the Confederates on July 24, 1864, and his meeting with the lady Major.

"At the battle of Peach Tree Creek, I got captured, and was brought before General Hood to be pumped; and as he could not get anything out of me, he had ordered me back to the other prisoners, when an officer attended by an escort, rode up and saluted the General.

"*Ha! Mademoiselle Major, how do you do?*" replied the General, doffing his hat.

"`Well, General'; and she jumped off her horse, throwing the bridle to her orderly, and politely returned the salute.

"The She-Major was strangely dressed; she wore a cap decked with feathers and gold lace, flowing pants, with a full kind of velvet coat coming just below her hips, and fastened with a rich crimson sash, and partly open at the bosom.

"In her belt she carried a revolver, and by her side a regulation sword. I looked at her; her features were rather sunburned, giving her a manly appearance. Only for her voluptuous bust, little hands, and peculiar airs, I might have taken her to be a very handsome little officer of the masculine gender.

"As I gazed at her, she looked full into my face; and turning to the General, she pointed her whip at me, and asked, `Who is that fellow, General?'

"'A prisoner that has just come in - a dunce; I couldn't get a word out of him.'

"'Indeed, General, that is a spy'; and she again pointed her whip at me.

"'Oh, no; he is only just brought in captured.'

"'That may be; but he is a spy. I saw him at General Johnston's one day and he was full of lying information, which cost the General many a life.'

"'Is that so?' said the General.

"'On my honor; come here, Hartly'; and she called over her orderly. 'Did you ever see that man before?'

"'Yes, Mademoiselle Major.'

"'Where?'

"'At General Johnston's, where he was giving information as a scout.'

"'What have you to say to all this, my man?' said the General.

"I had nothing to say, for it was true."

"'What shall I do with him; shall I hang him?' said the General.

"'Give him to me,' said she, with a sweet smile; 'I am going to General Johnston's; it might be well to take him there.'

"'I make you a present of him,' said the General.

"After spending some time with the General in the tent, she came out, and placing me between herself and her orderly, rode off. When she came into the wood, she and her orderly alighted, and she pulled out from under her dress a strong, but fine, rope.

"*'Sneaking dog of a Yankee!'* she exclaimed, looking at me with a vengeful eye, *'you hung the only man I ever loved; I swore I'd have vengeance. I have had it; but I have it doubly now, by giving you a similar death.'*

"My hands, all this time were firmly tied, so I was powerless. While the orderly stood with a pistol before me, she tied the rope firmly around my neck, giving it several good pulls, to make sure it was all right. They then helped me to get up on the saddle of one of the horses, so as to have a fall, while the orderly proceeded up the tree to tie the rope to a limb.

"Now was my time. While the orderly was climbing, I flung my two hands across the rope and snatched it from him, and drove my heels furiously into the horse's side, which made him plunge and rear. She held him bravely with one hand, while pulling out her pistol with the other. Before she could fire, I got a chance, and struck her with my heavy boot right in the face, spoiling her beauty, and giving the dentist a job. She fell. The horse bounded off with me, and I escaped." (29)

MANY WOMEN SERVED...
..on both sides in the Civil War.
-- *National Tribune*, Jan. 17, 1935

"CHARLES MARTIN"
(Soldier - Pa. Rgt)

A fair and sprightly girl, of but twelve dimpled summers, and giving the name of "Charles Martin", enlisted in one of the Pennsylvania regiments, in the early period of the war, as a drummer boy.

She had evidently enjoyed the advantage of education, could write a good hand, and even composed very well. She made herself useful to officers of the regiment in the capacity of a clerk; and though involved in the scenes and chances of no less than five battles, she escaped unwounded and unharmed.

The officers never dreamed of any hitch as to her sex. After a while, she was taken down sick with the typhoid fever, a disease then quite prevalent in Philadelphia, and was removed to Pennsylvania Hospital.

It was while there that the worthy matron of the institution discovered the drummer boy, who had passed through so many fatigues, perils and rough experiences, to be no more nor less than a girl not yet in her teens. ~~Quoted (24)

"FRANK MARTIN"
(Soldier - 8th MI, 2nd E. TN, 25th MI, 23rd KY)

In the spring of 1863, a Union Captain, accompanied by a young soldier apparently about seventeen years of age, arrived in Louisville, KY, in charge of some rebel prisoners.

During their stay in Louisville, the young soldier alluded to had occasion to visit head quarters, and at once attracted the attention of Colonel Marcellus Mundy, 23 KY Inf., as being exceedingly spright, and possessed of more than ordinary intelligence. Being in need of such a young man at Barracks No. 1, the Colonel detailed him for service in the institution. A few days subsequently, however, the startling secret was disclosed, that the supposed young man was a young lady, and the fact was established beyond doubt by a soldier who was raised in the same town with her and knew her parents. She acknowledged the "corn," and begged to be retained in the position to which she had been assigned; having been in the service ten months, she desired to serve during the war. Her wish was accordingly granted, and she remained at her post.

"Frank" was born near Bristol, PA., and she was raised in Allegheny City, the place of her parents' residence - highly respectable people, and in good circumstances. She was sent to a convent in Wheeling, Va, at twelve years of age, where she remained until the breaking out of the war, having acquired a [superior (40 p. 220-21)] / [military (24 p. 622)] education, and all the accomplishments of modern usage.

She visited home after leaving the convent, and after taking leave of her parents, proceeded to Louisville in July 1862, with the design of enlisting in the 2nd E. TN Cavalry, which she accomplished and accompanied the Army of the Cumberland to Nashville.

She was in the thickest of the fights at Murfreesboro and was severely wounded in the shoulder but fought gallantly and waded Stone river into Murfreesboro on the memorable Sunday on which our forces were driven back. She had her wound dressed, and here her sex was disclosed, and General Rosecrans being made acquainted with the fact.

"Frank" was accordingly mustered out of service, notwithstanding her earnest entreaty to be allowed to serve the cause she loved so well. The General was very favorably impressed with her daring bravery, and superintended the arrangements for her transmission to her parents.

She left the Army of the Cumberland, resolved to enlist again in the very first regiment she met. When she arrived at Bowling Green, therefore, she found the 8th MI there and enlisted and [remained until that regiment was mustered out of the service (40)] continued to share it's fortunes, being honored with position of regimental bugler. She was an excellent horseman; saw and bravely endured all the privations and hardships incident to the life of a soldier; and gained an enviable reputation as a scout, having made several remarkable expeditions which were attended with signal success.

Of only eighteen years of age, quite small, and a beautiful figure, "Frank" was a decided attraction. She had auburn hair which she wore quite short, and large blue eyes, beaming with intelligence. Her complexion, naturally very fair, became somewhat bronzed from exposure. In fine, she was exceedingly pretty and amiable. Her conversation denoted more than ordinary accomplishment, and what was stranger than all, she appeared very refined in her manners, giving no evidence whatever of the rudeness which might naturally be expected from her camp and field contacts.

The pretty bugler stated that *she had discovered a great many females in the army, and was intimately acquainted with one such - a young lady holding a commission as Lieutenant in the army. She had assisted in burying three female soldiers at different times, whose sex was unknown to any but herself.* ~~Quoted (24 p. 622);(40 p. 220-21) (See "THREE WHO DIED" and "FRANCES HOOK")

.....other Michigan heroines were .... an unknown in the 8th and in the 25th MI regiments who passed as **Frank Martin**...(30 p. 470)

Since we do not know FRANK MARTIN'S real name, the account of ELLA RENO has been inserted here due to similarities indicating they might be one in the same. (43 p. 42)

ELLA RENO
(Cavalryman 5th KY, 8th MI)

From the journal of Daniel Reed Larned, Library of Congress, May 14, 1863, Cincinnati, OH. [Larned was Burnside's private secretary.]

<u>Page 4, May 14, 1863</u> -"This morning a bit of nonsense comes up to disturb the regular routine of red tape. A cavalryman was sent to our headquarters on supposition that the duties he had been performing was not exactly those that legitimately belonged to his sex - on further examination he swore that his name was Miss ELLA RENO.

"She had been serving for 18 months in a Kentucky Cavalry regiment - and was noted for her bravery and daring. She proves to be a niece of our lamented General Reno. She was delivered over to the wife of one of our orderlies who will see her properly dressed when she will be sent to her home. She says she has been sent home three times before, but always managed to get back to the army."

Page 8, May 15, 1863 - "Miss Ella Reno (our soger boy) came into see the General this morning. She was dressed in her own clothes, with a straw flat; her face was brown, her hair cut short army fashion. She was about the average size and not a bad looking woman. How she ever passed for a man, I can't see."

"She served four months as a private in the 5th Kentucky Cavalry - was then transferred by her own request to the 8th Michigan Infantry, and has done all the duties of ordinary private; made long marches, been in hot battles, stood guard, been out on picket duty, and was [admonished?] for telling her superior officer that 'if he was not more loyal he had better take off his stripes, throw up his commission and go home,' - was put in prison and did prison duty two weeks, went out foraging on a mule, was ordered to take a train of wagons around a river at night which she accomplished."

"She wants to go back to the army but says she won't if the General advises her not to; so he has got her a place in the hospital at Louisville. She cooks well and is very lady like in her appearance."

[Note: *Ella is also mentioned in William Marvel's "BURNSIDE", by Univ. of NC Press, 1991, in which he states that Ella was probably with Willcox* and the 8th MI on South Mountain when Maj. General Jesse L. Reno died, 14 Sep 1862.*] (Courtesy: *Pat Brennan*); (* see also Maj. Lyman G. Willcox, 3rd MI Cav., and Col. Orlando B. Willcox, 1st MI Inf., per Historical Register and Dictionary of the U.S. Army, Vol. II, Gov't. Printing Office, Washington, 1903)

MARION McKENZIE
aka Harry Fitzallen
(Soldier-5th VA)

Born in Nashville, Tenn, [some accounts say she was borne in Scotland and raised in New York], Marion was living in her aunt's boarding house in Cincinnati, when she made her way to Gallipolis (OH) and intercepted the 5th, enroute from Wheeling (W)Va, to the upper Kanawah Valley. Of dubious moral intent, Marion soon became acquainted with many of the fun-loving boys. Pooling their resources, they put together a uniform for her and presented her as the new recruit "Harry Fitzallen". She was accepted, and provided with a horse. Eventually she was detected and sent by boat to Atheneum Prison.

In a letter dated Jan 5, 1863 to the Commissary General of Prisons, from Provost Marshal, Maj. Joseph Darr, Jr.:

"...I respectfully suggest .... she be sent if possible, to some house of refuge or detention and be held there until the end of the rebellion....(she) refuses to wear women's clothing as purchased for her. .... but clings to the cavalry pea-jacket and pantaloons in which she soldiered through the Kanawah Valley..." (14)

The Official Records state that she was a former actress, and joined a Kentucky regiment in 1861, for "love of excitement". She was twenty years old, very short and very thick - and well-educated. After she was arrested in Charles Town for spying in 1861, she requested that she and Mary Jane Green be sent to the Cincinnati House for Refugees, but the request was denied and they were sent to the Old Capitol Prison. She served in several other regiments after detection.

MINNESOTA GIRL
(Soldier)

Being wounded nearly always ended the service of a woman in disguise. Such was common, as in the case of a young girl from Minnesota who claimed to have already served successfully for two years. Her identity is not known. (22)

MIRRORS AND SILKS
(Soldiers - C.S.A.)

Mirrors and silk dresses were hard to come by during the war, and several Confederate soldier-women (while foraging) betrayed their disguises by fighting over them.

MISSION ACCOMPLISHED
(Soldier - Indiana Rgt.)

There was in one of the Indiana regiments a young girl who did soldier's service for the space of two years, and all under the most peculiar circumstances - never until the last disclosing her sex. Having, at the end of the period named, got tired of the rough and arduous life she was leading, she procured a supply of feminine apparel, and arraying herself therein, set off for home, after calling on her Colonel, telling who she was and bidding him good-by -- leaving him and all the rest of the officers, as well as the men, who became aware of her identity, utterly dumb with amazement.

She had fought bravely, and had done her duty well, all through the two years she had been in the service, and had received two severe wounds, but during all this period her sex was undiscovered. Her reason for entering the service was that she might be near a young man whom she loved; but he proving a coward, she became disgusted with him, and then continued to serve in the hope that some friendly bullet would end her unhappy life. But finally becoming cured of her love, romance and misanthropy, she concluded to return to her proper sphere in life and live like a rational creature. ~~Quoted (24)

MADILINE MOORE

MADILINE MOORE
(Soldier Lieutenant)

Madiline is believed to have been awarded a Lieutenants' commission as a man. She was in the Cavalry and led a charge in the Battle of the Wilderness. Like many others, she followed her lover to war and put on the uniform of a fallen officer to effect her disguise.(42)

~~~~~~~~~~~~~~~~~~~~~~~~~~~~~~~~~~~~~

SUE MUNDAY
aka Lieutenant Flowers
(Guerrilla - KY)

A band of guerrillas, lead by a notorious character named Berry, formerly of John Morgan's command, attacked the stage near Shawneetown, KY, one Friday evening, robbing the passengers and rifling the mail bag. After this exploit, the band moved in the direction of Harrodsburg, relieved the toll-gate keeper near that place of cash and various articles, and then dashed into town.

The Savings Bank was honored with the first call. The managers of the institution observed the movement, and hastily closed and barred the doors before the scoundrels could gain an entrance. The robbers fired several shots as the doors were being closed, but no injury was done by the same. Finding they could not force the doors, the guerrillas proposed to fire the building, but before they could put the design into execution, the citizens, who had armed themselves and collected to defend their homes, commenced firing on the robber band. The outlaws were taken by surprise and greatly alarmed, fled from the town.

One of the peculiar characters or personages composing this band of cut-throats, was the officer second in command, recognized by the men as "Lieutenant Flowers". The officer in question was a young woman, her real name being Sue Munday. She dressed herself in male attire, generally sporting a full Confederate uniform. Upon her head she wore a jaunty plumed hat, beneath which there escaped a wealth of dark brown hair, falling around and down her shoulders in luxuriant curls. She was possessed of a comely form, had a dark piercing eye, was a bold rider and daring leader. Prior to connecting herself with Berry's gang of outlaws, she was associated with the band commanded by Captain Alexander, who met his doom some time previously in Southern Kentucky.

Lieutenant Flowers, or Sue Munday, was a practiced robber, and many ladies, who had been so unfortunate as to meet her on the highway, could testify with what [boldness] she presented a pistol and commanded, "stand and deliver." Her name had become widely known, and to the ladies, it was associated with horror. On the evening when the outlaws were at Harrodsburg, Sue dexterously robbed a young lady of her watch and chain, and if the citizens had not so unceremoniously expelled the thieving band from the town, she would doubtless have paid her respects to the jewelry and valuables of all the ladies of the place.

The operations of Sue Munday, the female guerrilla, will long be remembered in Kentucky. About the middle of October, 1864, Sue in company with Captain Berry, made a descent at the head of their marauding gang, upon Jeffersontown, and took possession of the place. Sue Munday dismounted at the Davis House and had her canteen filled with whisky. A negro boy was mounted on a horse, armed in the most complete manner, and rode with the gang. He stood guard over the horses, while the scoundrels were scattered about the town engaged in robbing people. The discharge of fire arms was heard by several parties residing in the vicinity, but they were ignorant of the cause.

A short time, however, after these reports were heard, Mr. James Simpson, on his way to Jeffersontown, was met in the road by the outlaws and robbed of 27 dollars in money. He observed that Sue Munday's pistol was empty, and the fresh stains showed that it had very recently been discharged. While Mr. S. was being robbed, she was engaged in reloading her revolver. She pointed the muzzle at the breast of Mr. S., and smiled with fiendish satisfaction at his embarrassment as she capped the tube of each barrel of the cylinder. After being released, Mr. S. rode directly to Jeffersontown and related his adventure. He was informed that, with the prisoner in Federal uniform, the party numbered eight when in town. He met but seven on the road and no prisoners.

The citizens at once surmised that the soldier had been murdered, and following the trail of the guerrillas, they approached the dark ravine, and found their worst apprehensions too true. His body was marked with five pistolshot wounds, and two deep stabs, as if made by the keen blade of a dagger. All the circumstances went to prove that the murder was committed by one hand, and that hand Sue Munday's the outlaw woman, and the wild daring leader of the band.

By a record in a small memorandum book, found upon the dead body, it was learned that the name of the murdered man was Hugh Wilson. Upon his person was also found a letter dated Mt. Vernon, Ill., and presumed to be from his wife, as it commenced with "My dear husband,". She wrote in an affectionate manner and spoke with loving fondness of their pleasant home and the little darling ones who `sent love to pa.' This letter was found in his bosom, pierced by balls and stained with blood gushed in warm lifestreams from his heart. ~~Quoted (24)

The "NANCIES"
Women's Home Guard
LaGrange, GA

The women of Castroville had nothing over the ladies in Troup County, GA. They formed their own home guard, and called it the "Nancy Harts" *(not the same as the one previously mentioned in this manuscript)* in honor of a "Georgia heroine of the American Revolution who successfully defended her home against the British."

The women were armed with rifles and muskets and made their own ammunition. They drilled twice a week, and held target practice and parades to inspire more confidence. Mrs. J. Brown Morgan was elected Captain.

The war came to their door just after the fall of West Point, April, 1865, when Colonel LaGrange (coincidentally the same name) entered the town. The "Nancies" confronted the Colonel, his men, and about 100 prisoners in the middle of the street in front of the LaGrange Female's Campus. The Colonel assured the women he did not want to fight them, or destroy their homes. Instead, the women entertained the Federal officers and their Confederate prisoners that evening. The next day, only the tannery, steam mill, a tin shop, and the depot were burned.

(See: "History of Troup County", by Clifford Smith, 1933; "A History of LaGrange, GA 1828-1900" and "Genealogical and Historical Register of Troup Co., GA", Forrest Clark Johnson III, Family Tree Publishers, 1987, p. 70-73) Courtesy *Sandra Smith*

NEW ORLEANS
(Soldier - 14th ME Vol.)

One of the recruits who enlisted at New Orleans proved to be a woman and did duty until about the close of the war. She was small and slightly built and for that reason was excused from some heavy fatigue duty. She was very plain looking and had informed me that she had worked at tailoring; and she used to do mending for me very nicely.

She enlisted in New Orleans with her lover and was with him until discharged from the service. I did not learn of her sex till the close of the war. If I had been anything but a boy, I should probably have seen from her form that she was a female.

~~Quoted, Capt.& Brvt Lt Col Ira B.Gardner,"*Recollections of the 14th Maine Vol., Co.I, 1862-1865*"

NORTH ANNA
(Soldier - CSA)

The following report was issued by O.B. Curtis, of the 24th Michigan, relative to an incident at the North Anna Campaign on May 26, 1864, and further detailed in a letter from a Union engineer, Andrew Crossley on May 29:

"A woman was captured dressed as a Confederate soldier."
---Curtis

"She was mounted just like a man and belonged to cavalry though she was taken as a spy. She wore her hair long and did not like to have our men looking at her. Some men stopped to look at her as she went by us and she picked up rocks and threw at them." ---Crossley (33)

"CHARLES NORTON"
(Soldier - 141st PA Vol.)

While in Camp Curtin there came into the quarters of Co. E, a bright, black-eyed boy who gave his name as Charles Norton, and desiring to go to the front offered his services to Captain Reeves as servant. The Captain was favorably impressed with the appearance of the little fellow and employed him. He was a faithful and efficient helper at Headquarters, always marching with his company and keeping a sharp lookout for the officers' property.

Among his other qualifications he was a splendid cook, preparing little dainties from the slender stock the commissary afforded, so that Captain Reeves' mess enjoyed many delicacies the other officers knew nothing of. The boy of course became a general favorite.

When the Captain became sick at Poolesville, Charlie staid at his side and tenderly cared for him, and returned to camp with him and resumed his duties at Headquarters where he continued until the battle of Chancellorsville, where an incident occurred that disclosed the fact that Charlie Norton was a woman.

Captain Mercur had a delicate foot and wore a boot unusually small for a man. One morning he awoke to find his boots missing. He could get no trace of them for several days but finally discovered them on Norton's feet. He had never seen a man before who could wear his boots, and on questioning Norton, accused him flatly of stealing which he at first denied but afterward confessed.

In the course of the investigation the Captain's cook proved to be of the opposite sex, and it is needless to add was speedily mustered out of the service. Some of the members of that company have seen her since and talked with her in regard to this somewhat romantic adventure. She said she was deeply interested in the war, and desired to serve her country in some way, and was obliged to assume the disguise she adopted in order to carry out her plan.

~~Quoted, Chaplain David Craft, "History of the 141st PA Vol." 1862-1865.

OHIO GIRL
(Soldier - 3rd Ohio)

The lover of a young Ohio girl had enlisted, and she determined to join him. She was inspected, accepted, and sworn in with the rest of the company; marched to Camp Jackson, Ohio, drilled there several days, when she was sent with the Third Ohio Regiment to Camp Dennison, near Cincinnati. Here she assisted in all the duties of forming a new camp, handling lumber, standing sentry, etc., until Saturday, when ascertaining for the first time that there were TWO Camp Dennisons, and that while she was in one her lover was in the other, in Lancaster, Penna.

She went to Colonel Morrow, and requested to be changed from the company she was in, giving as her reason that she preferred associating with Americans, as her company was composed of Irishmen. Her real design was, when her request should be granted, to choose a place in one of the companies of the Second Regiment, not knowing that it would be impossible to change her from one regiment to another.

Colonel Morrow discovered the secret of her sex. Marshal Thompson then supplied her with clothing, having enrobed herself in which, she expressed a desire to leave, as she had friends in the city with whom she could sojourn. She was released. ~~ Quoted (24)

CORNELIA OLDOM
(Heroine)

A marauding band of secessionists in Kentucky, on their way to Mount Sterling, stopped at the house of Mr. Oldom and, he being absent at the time, plundered him of all his horses, and among them a valuable one belonging to his daughter, Cornelia.

She resisted the outrage as long as she could, but finding all her efforts in vain, she sprang upon another horse and started post haste toward the town to give the alarm. Her first animal gave out, when she seized another, and meeting the messenger from Middletown, she sent him as fast as his horse could carry him to convey the necessary warning to Mount Sterling where he arrived most opportunely.

Miss Oldom then retraced her way toward home, taking with her a double-barreled shotgun. She found a pair of saddlebags on the road belonging to a Confederate officer, which contained a pair of revolvers, and soon she came up with the advancing marauders and ordered them to halt.

Perceiving that one of the thieves rode her horse, she ordered him to surrender the animal; this he refused, and finding that persuasion would not gain her ends, she levelled the shotgun at the rider, commanding him, "down from his horse," and threatened to fire if he did not comply. Her indomitable spirit at last prevailed, and the robbers, seeing something in her eye that spoke a terrible menace, surrendered her favorite steed.

When she had regained his back, and patted him on the neck, he gave a neigh of mingled recognition and triumph, and she turned his head homeward and cantered off as leisurely as if she were taking her morning exercise. ~~Quoted (24)

ROSE O'NEAL Greenhow
(Confederate Spy)

Rose, aunt of Mrs. Stephen A. Douglas was a prominent member of Washington Society. At forty four years of age she was popular among the most influential politicians. Charming and mysterious, she had no trouble gathering the information she sought.

Transmitting messages to Beauregard's staff by secret code, she informed the South of many of the North's military plans. Eventually she was caught, however and imprisoned in her own home for a time, then was moved to Old Capitol Prison in Jan. '62, taking her small daughter, Rose, to prison with her.

Immediately upon her release from prison, she headed South to meet with Southern officials then on to France. With little Rose tucked safely away in a convent, she headed on to England where she was granted an audience with Queen Victoria.

On September 30, 1864, she sailed without Rose, back to the Southern shores of the United states, where her ship ran aground off Wilmington, NC. She was drowned when a wave overturned the small boat that was carrying her to shore from the grounded ship. She was considered a heroine to the South, and so buried with military honors.

Little is known of young Rose except that she later took up the acting profession. (22),(28)

ONE HUNDRED FIFTY RECRUITS
Mary Jane G_____

A Washington correspondent said the official records of the military authorities in that city show that **upward of one hundred and fifty female recruits** have been discovered, and made to resume the garments of their sex.

It is supposed that nearly all of these were in collusion with men who were examined by the surgeons and accepted, after which the fair ones substituted themselves and came on to the war.

Curiously enough, *over seventy* of these martial demoiselles, when their sex was discovered, were acting as officers' servants. *In one regiment there are seventeen* officers' servants, in blue blouses and pants, who had to be clothed in calico and crinoline.

Even a general, who has won many laurels in the war, had a handsome, fresh looking "detailed man" acting as his clerk, whose real name turned out to be Mary Jane G____, and who has parents in Trenton who are estimable members of society. She said in excuse that she `wanted to see the world'.~~Quoted, *INDEPENDENT REPUBLICAN*, Goshen, NY, June 20, 1864

~~~~~~~~~~~~~~~~~~~~~~~~~~~~~~~~~~~~

MARY OWENS
aka John Evans
(Soldier - Penna.)

An undaunted woman was Mary Owens. This remarkable person accompanied her husband to the army, fought by his side until he fell by the hand of his country's enemy, [she being wounded in the same battle] and then [she] returned home in full uniform, to tell the adventurous tale of her devotion and sufferings.

She was in the service eighteen months, took part in three battles, and was wounded twice, - first in the face above the right eye, and then in her arm; this required her to be taken to the hospital where she was obliged to confess her true sex and the circumstances of her being in the ranks.

She had enlisted in the town of Danville, Montour Co., PA, under the name of John Evans, and gave as her reason for such a romantic and hazardous undertaking, the fact that her father was uncompromising in his hostility to her marriage with Mr. Owens, threatening violence in case she disobeyed his commands: whereupon, after having been secretly married, she donned the United States uniform, enlisted in the same company with her husband, endured all the hardships of the camp, and the dangers of the field, saw her husband fall dead by her side, and returned home wounded and a widow - young, rather pretty, and of course, the heroine of the neighborhood.

Though of Welsh parentage, she was a genuine Yankee in patriotism and "smartness".~~Quoted (24)

MELVERINA ELVERINA PEPPERCORN
(Soldier - C.S.A./TN)

You probably never heard of Alexander "the Great" Peppercorn, but he had a twin sister who thought in 1862, that he was great enough to follow into battle. The first of the twins to be born, sister Melverina boasted that she was "... older than Lexy ..." and could "... shoot just as well ...".

In the first battle they fought together, Alexander received a leg wound and Melverina acted as his nurse until he recovered. Conflicting reports say they then returned to the Army, where another report says that was her only battle.

One report indicates that Lee had surrendered before she had the chance to re-enlist. (32)

MARY ANN PERKINS
MADAME BOIVERT
(Confederate Vivandieres)

These two ladies were entered on the roll of the Gardes Lafayette from Mobile. (27)

GEORGIANNA PETERMAN
(Soldier - 7th WI)

The Plattville, Wis., "*WITNESS*", of March 1864, records, "Miss Peterman has been for two years a drummer in the Seventh Wisconsin. She lives in Ellenboro, Wis., is about twenty years old, wears soldier clothes, and is quiet and reserved."

These half-soldier heroines generally adopted a semi-military dress, and became expert in the use of the rifle, and skillful shots. (16 p. 119);(23 p. 95)

BELLE PETERSON
(Soldier - Wisc.)

A letter of *L.D. Culver*, Ellenboro, Wisc., dated May 1910, tells of Belle Peterson, a local country girl who left home to join the army. The approximate date of her enlistment was late 1862, and she served for some time. No one suspected she was a girl. (See: Hurn's "Wisconsin Women in the War", Madison, 1911) *Courtesy Eleanor Hoffman*

MRS. PHELPS
(Heroine)

John F. Phelps, a loyal Missourian, resided near Wilson's Creek, where the bloody engagement took place [on the 9th/10th of August] in which General Lyon [already twice wounded] met his untimely but heroic death. At the time of the battle he was away from home, in command of a Union regiment of Missouri Volunteers.

After Lyon's death the Union force retreated to Springfield, leaving the body of their general in the hands of the enemy. Mrs. Phelps determined to rescue it, and see that it had a Christian burial. It was reported also that some of the secessionists had threatened to cut out the heart of the dead soldier, and preserve it as a trophy.

Arming herself, she went out on the field, appalling as it was with the dead still unburied, and stood guard over the body of the hero all night. When ordered to give it up, she fearlessly refused; and when they insisted, she said they must sacrifice her before they could lay hands on the remains of that fallen brave.

After daylight she made the proper arrangements, and removed the corpse to her house, where it was duly laid out. To furnish him a funeral pall, she cut into breadths and sewed together in a proper form, a magnificent black velvet robe, a part of her own apparel.

Though perfectly aware of her unprotected situation, the rebels surrounded the house in which the lifeless form of a gallant enemy was guarded by a solitary but heroic woman, and made the night hideous by savage screams, horrible oaths, and barbarous threats. In a short time however, they retreated, and the body of General Lyon was taken in charge by the army, removed to Connecticut, his native state, and there interred with the fullest military honors. ~~Quoted (15 p. 503-09).

It was later discovered that General Lyon, a bachelor of means, had bequeathed about thirty thousand dollars to the war effort. It was all that he possessed. (30 p. 4);(31 p. 163)

BETTIE TAYLOR PHILIPS
("Mother" of the "Orphan Brigade")

Individual deeds of daring and endurance by the women of the South may be given almost indefinitely. Such is the story of Mrs. Philips, of Kentucky.

Mrs. Philips was born in Morganfield, KY, April 6, 1830. She was the daughter of Mary Rives and Dr. Gibson Berry Taylor, both natives of Virginia. In 1847 she was married to W. D. Philips, who, at the very beginning of the war, entered the Southern army.

In the fall of 1861, Mrs. Philips joined her husband at Bowling Green, KY, where he had received the appointment of Quartermaster to the 4th KY Regiment, Hanson's Brigade, Breckinridge's Division. Later, after the death of the heroic Hanson, it was commanded by General Joe Lewis, and has come down to fame as the "Orphan Brigade".

Mrs. Philips, having no children, determined to follow the fortunes of her husband through weal or woe. She remained at his side through all the stern vicissitudes of war, in camp, on long marches, often under shot and shell of the enemy, but ever at hand as an angel of mercy. At Shiloh, at Donelson, and many other hard-fought fields of the South, she ministered to the sick, wounded, and dying of her beloved brigade.

Then, after two years of the hardships incident to camp life, her health, which had never been robust, failed, but not the dauntless spirit of this brave woman. She was advised to rest; so she started from a point in Tennessee for her home in Kentucky.

At Nashville, she was arrested, and two rough soldiers were commissioned to search her person for weapons and concealed papers. They told her their mission and started to execute the order.

"*Stop where you are!*" she cried, and drew her pistol, "*I will never submit to the humiliation of being searched by men. Send a woman to me.*" Awed by her courage, they retreated, and returned with a woman who made the most rigid search of her person.

She was then sent to Louisville and tried as a spy; but as there was no evidence to convict her, she was finally acquitted and sent back through the lines and left in a lonely forest in Tennessee.

After wandering for many miles, this frail and delicate little woman reached a road and was mercifully taken up by a passing countryman in a wagon and conveyed to the nearest railroad station. She soon reached the shelter of the camp, her home, and never was there any more joyful homecoming! Every man in the command begged the honor of shaking her hand; the band played "Home Again," and strong men wept.

Mrs. Philips remained with the brigade until the close of the war, then returned to her home in Uniontown. She devoted the few remaining years of her life to the cause of the South, and was instrumental in erecting the soldier's monument at Morganfield.
~~Quoted (17)

PICKETT'S DIVISION
(Soldier - C.S.A.)

Elsewhere in this manuscript is an account of a woman killed in Pickett's Charge at Gettysburg. But it would appear that there were other women in the battle as indicated by the report of a woman who was killed in battle alongside her husband, in that same charge about July 3, 1863. They were found together where they died, on Cemetery Ridge. (32) (See: *Killed in Pickett's Charge*)

MARY ANN PITMAN
aka Lieutenant Rawley
(Soldier - C.S.A.)

This young woman from Chestnut Bluff, Tennessee, won her place in women's history by earning a Lieutenant's commission while disguised as Lt. Rawley, under Forrest's command.

Official service records show that Lt. Rawley was an effective witness in 1864 during a hearing in which the Sons of Liberty were investigated relative to conspiring to overthrow the U.S. government. (32)

ANTOINETTE POLK
(Heroine)

Antoinette was from Columbia, Tennessee, and gained some notariety for her successful assistance to escaping Confederate soldiers.

In an interesting turn of events, she later married a man who fought for the Union. He was the Baron de Charette, who took her to Brittany to live on the family estate. (22)

ELLIE M. POOL
aka Stewart
(Guerrilla/Reporter)

Some of the lady guerrillas were very intelligent, in opposite to some of the inmates of the Atheneum Prison. One of these was Miss Ellie M. Poole, a reporter for the Richmond Enquirer and the Baltimore Exchange. She traveled through the Ohio Valley, using the name of "Stewart" until her actions became suspicious and she was incarcerated in the Atheneum Prison.

Major Darr underestimated Ellie. That night she made a long rope from bed sheets and escaped from the second floor of the prison. The persistant reporter and perhaps a spy was again arrested within ten miles of enemy lines in Kentucky and returned to Atheneum. She had $7,500 in her possession and that was enough to convict her in those nervous times.~~Quoted (14)

A POPULAR GIRL
(Heroine)

Many women, most of whom will never be identified, went to great risk of life to aid escaping soldiers, both North and South and still were able to maintain their popularity with both.

One such young lady in East Tennessee, assisted Junius Henri Browne and his newspaper colleagues in escaping from a Confederate prison. Then, acting as their guide, led them to safety. (22)

PRISONERS

...other [West] Virginia Partisan Ranger ladies from the Little Kanawah Valley had been arrested and sent to the Atheneum Prison in Wheeling, where they were charged with treason:

DORA and JULIA DUNBAR, AMANDA and BELLE GOSHORN, ELIZA C. HUGHES, ELIZABETH PHILLIPS, and HANNAH and JOANNA SMITH.

Despite the treason charge, Governor Pierpont sent them to Camp Chase in Columbus...

One of his lady prisoners from the mountains, **MARY JANE PRATHER** ... decided she would add one more [baby] to her family in July, and Pierpont did not want that to happen in his ... prison. ... He suggested to the prison authorities in Washington that they dispose of the female prisoners by legal parole at City Point, on the James River in Virginia. That was done.

Letter from Wm. Hoffman to Major Darr:

"Major, please deliver to the Provost Marshal in this city [Wheeling], **MARY J. GREEN, MARIAH [Margaret ?] MURPHY**, of Braxton Co., and **JENNIE DeHART**, female prisoners now in your custody, charged with disloyal offenses.

If there are any charges of disloyalty against **MARION McKENZIE** or MARY JANE PRATHER you will send them also. Wearing soldier's clothing in camp is not an offense for which they can be sent South..."

"**ELIZABETH HAYS** and **MARY SUMMERS** are very hard cases and will have to remain in your hands until you can see a good opening to dispose of them which I hope will soon present itself." [also in uniform]

It iscertain that **MARY JANE GREEN, KATE BROWN, NANCY HART,** and others, worked with the guerrilla captains in the counties of Braxton, Webster, Lewis, Wirt, Calhoun and Wood [W.Va].

One of the troublemakers at Atheneum Prison was a **Mrs. Ba(g)xley,** who complained constantly about the living quarters. A dedicated Confederate, she refused to sleep under an army blanket marked U.S. ~~Quoted (14)

PRIVATE CLAPP'S GIRLFRIEND
(7th Maine)

When the Seventh Maine regiment were encamped in Baltimore in the summer of 1861, one of the soldiers named Clapp, fell in love with a young girl who used to peddle apples to the boys, and promised to marry her. Her mother consented, but about the time set for the marriage the regiment left the place.

After they had been in their new location on the Potomac about three weeks, who should come into camp one day but Clapp's girl! After a week or so the captain of Clapp's company gave his consent, and they were married and had a tent to themselves. But she was a foolish thing, and after a while the Colonel and Captain wanted to get rid of her.

It happened that Clapp was one of the men detached from his regiment to go on board the Western gunboats. So his wife packed up and was going back to Baltimore. But as luck would have it, when Clapp presented himself at headquarters, they wouldn't accept him, and sent him back to camp. When the time came for the regiment to leave camp, and it started on the advance, they all supposed that was the last they should see of the soldier's girl.

But one fine day who should march into camp at its new quarters but Mrs. Clapp, dressed in full military suit, with a knapsack on her back and canteenand haversack by her side! She was indeed a romantic feminine on a `bender'. Her disguise was seen through at once, and she was sent to the guard house, to be from there sent back to Washington. ~~Quoted (24)

PROVOST GUARD

Whether they were offficially recognized or not, it is obvious by the following that women participated in official capacities in a variety of branches of the military service. It was reported that when Varina (Mrs. Jefferson) Davis boarded a ship for Savannah, she had to submit to a baggage search by the provost guard. The detectives who searched her baggage were women. (19)

IDA REMINGTON
(Soldier - 11th NY)

The *Detroit Advertiser and Tribune,* on Aug.27, 1863, related the account in Harrisburg, PA, of the arrest of a Rochester, NY, soldier suspected of being a woman. She confessed to the truth, and gave the police her name. Her regiment had been sent to Pennsylvania for the Gettysburg campaign.

She'd been in major battles for two years, including South Mountain and Antietam and had been personal servant to a Captain.

They locked her up, but after a second hearing, she was released and left town.

BELLE REYNOLDS

MAJOR BELLE REYNOLDS
(Officer's Wife-Heroine)
17th IL, Co. A

"As I was one of the very few ladies [nurses] who were present at the battle [of Shiloh], and had witnessed so large a portion of its scenes, the story seemed to interest all who heard, and someone suggested, 'She deserves a commission more than half the officers.' 'Let's make one, "*said another. No sooner said, than a blank commission was brought, and the governor directed his secretary to fill it out, giving me the rank of a major."*

"This was done: the name of the governor, of Adjutant Fuller, and the Secretary of State were added, the Seal of the State of Illinois was appended, and the parchment handed me, with many congratulations. I received it, not so much as an honor which I really deserved, but simply as an acknowledgment of merit for having done what I could." ---**Belle Reynolds** ~Quoted (15)

Governor Yates, of Illinois, paid a rather unusual but well merited compliment to Mrs. Reynolds, wife of Lt Reynolds, Co A, 17th Ill, and a resident of that city. [The citizens of Peoria, her home town, were so impressed with the honor that they formally thanked the Governor.(23)]

Mrs. Reynolds accompanied her husband through the greater part of the campaigns through which the Seventeenth passed, sharing with him the dangers and privations of a soldier's life [sometimes carrying a musket on her shoulder (23)]. She was present at the battle of Pittsburgh Landing, and like a ministering angel attended to the wants of as many of the wounded and dying soldiers as she could, thus winning the gratitude and esteem of the brave fellows by whom she was surrounded.~Quoted (24)

Belle was born Arabella L. Macomber, on October 20, 1840, in Shelburne Falls, Mass. Later her family moved to Iowa where Belle taught in the first Cass County school while still a teenager.

Belle married William S. Reynolds on April 19, 1860 - one year before the attack on Fort Sumpter. They received word of the attack while sitting in a little church in Peoria, Ill. William enlisted immediately, and Belle prepared to follow. She joined him at Bird's Point, Missouri, about three months later.

She served with her husband throughout his service into the Spring of 1864, ever sacrificing her own comforts for the care of the sick and wounded. When they returned to Peoria, Belle furthered her medical training in Chicago, as the student of Dr. Ludlam. Belle began to practice medicine professionally and served as resident physician at the Home for the Friendless in Chicago. In later years, Belle moved to Santa Barbara, California, and was still practicing medicine there in 1929. (From Illinois State Historical Library) (23)

"WILLIAM E. RILEY"
(Soldier - 15th IN Battery)

The *National Tribune* of May 25, 1899 gives a long account of a "strange character" who was a dashing artillerist that had passed into military service without a physical exam.

SACRAMENTO, KY

... Colonel [N.B.] Forrest and his men - armed principally with double-barrelled shot guns - were ordered to the headquarters of General Lloyd Tilghman at Hopkinsville, Kentucky. At the village of Sacramento, however, Forrest decided to overtake and attack a body of Federal cavalry.

Riding into action, a Kentucky girl, mounted on a superfine horse, galloped at his side and cheered his rangers forward. "*Her untied tresses,*" he wrote in his official report, "*floated in the breeze, infused nerve into my arm and kindled knightly chivalry in my heart.*" He seized a rifle from one of the volunteers and fired the first shot of the engagement.

He charged with no particular order other than a command for his troops to hold all fire until they were within close range; ... and he developed his famous movement by flank and rear ... Forrest, standing in his stirrups, his sabre in the air, seemed to be a foot taller than any other man in the world. The Federal cavalry broke and fled. ~~Quoted (19 p. 210)

SALLIE
(11th PA)

A real trooper was tough little Sallie. She marched from Fredericksburg to face Lee at Gettysburg. During the confusion she was separated from her comrades. Unable to catch up with them, she lay down among the dead and wounded to wait for those still living to come for her. Weak and ill when found, she was carried back to camp and nursed to health. Rallying, she went with the troops in the Overland Campaign of May 1864, where she was wounded in the neck.

Rallying again from her wound, she continued through battle after battle until Hatcher's Run in February, 1865. In the midst of battle, she was felled by a minie ball in the head. On the Gettysburg monument placed by the veterans of the 11th PA, is a likeness of Sallie - their brave little mascot dog. (13 p. 566) [Note: Though Sallie was an animal, it was important to the men of the 11th PA to acknowledge her. Her story is also told by the tour guides at Gettysburg National Battlefield Park, and they refer to her as "Sallie Ann".]

~~~~~~~~~~~~~~~~~~~~~~~~~~~~~~~~~~

LOLA SANCHEZ
(Confederate Courier)

Cuban Lola Sanchez lived with her family near Palatka, Florida. With strong sympathies for the South the whole family served in some way, both in the Confederate army and in the conveying of any useful information on Union activities.

With their mother an invalid, their brother at war, and their father in prison for spying, the chore of preparing refreshments for Union officers fell to the young ladies of the house. It was during such an evening that Lola overheard the officers discussing two upcoming raids against the south, and a foraging expedition.

Apparently unaware of the loyalties of the Sanchez family, the Union officers were oblivious to the plans being made right under their noses. Lola insructed one sister to entertain them, and another sister to keep their minds on food. The officers thus distracted, Lola was able to set about her mission to notify the Confederate troops.

It was not an easy trip as there were many obstacles of nature to overcome. She had to find her way through a dense forest, struggle through a tangle of vines, and wade across a stream. In spite of the perils, she was able to successfully deliver her message and return to the house in less than two hours - without the Union officers having been aware of her absence. The next day resulted in a victory for the South. (27 p. 379)

EMMA SANSOM
(Scout)

The story of Emma's adventure has been told over and over, and lives on as one of the favorites of the Civil War. For her bravery, the State of Alabama gave her a medal in 1864, and promised her land, which she claimed in 1899. That same year she was lauded in a ballad, written by John T. Moore. Later, in Gadsden, a marble statue of Emma was erected. Only fifteen years old, she bravely led N.B. Forrest and his men to a safe crossing in Black Creek, after the bridge had been burned. (22 p. 104)

Emma ... was born at Social Circle, in Ga. In 1852 her father had moved to Black Creek, Alabama, and he died there seven years later. [She had six brothers serving the Confederacy and she lived at home with her mother and sister.]

... Forrest asked where he could cross the creek; Emma explained about the ford ... Forrest told her "get up here behind me." ... Emma ... obeyed ... [nearing the ford] they both dismounted and crept through the bushes ... Emma [in the lead].

... Forrest quickly stepped between her and the Yankees. "I am glad to have you for a pilot ... but I am not going to make breastworks of you." The howitzers and muskets were firing fast then, Emma pointed out where Forrest must cross the water and they returned to the house.

[Before departing] Bedford Forrest asked Emma her name [and] for a lock of her hair. [He left her the following note:]

> "Hed Quaters in
> Sadle
> May 2, 1863
>
> "My highest regards to Miss Emma Sansom for her gallant conduct while my posse was skirmishing with the Federals across Black Creek Near Gadsden Alabama.
> N.B. Forrest
> Bry Genrl
> Com. N. Ala--"

~Quoted (19)

MISS SCHWARTZ
(Heroine)

In the summer of 1863, a party of guerrillas went in the night to the house of Mr.Schwartz, twelve miles from Jefferson City, Missouri, and on demanding admittance, were refused by Miss Schwartz, a girl of fifteen years.

They answered that they would come in, and commenced breaking down the door. Five or six men who were in the house, [Mr. Schwartz, John Wise, Capt. Golden - a government horse dealer, and a young man in his employ (24)] now ran out by the back door, taking with them, as they supposed, all the firearms (leaving the young girl to face the guerrillas alone).

In their haste, a revolver was left behind. The heroic girl seized it, and pointing it at the head of the leader of the gang, said - "*Come on, if you want to; some of you shall fall, or I will!*" The men told her they would kill her if she did not leave the door. She answered, "*The first man of you that takes a step towards this door dies. This is the home of my parents, my brothers and sisters, and I am able to and shall, defend it.*" After a brief consultation, the ruffians left. Brigadier-General Brown, in a general order, concludes as follows: --

"*It is with feelings of no common pride and pleasure that the commanding general announces this occurrence to the citizens and soldiers of his district. On the other hand, those miserable cowards who deserted this brave girl in the hour of danger, flying from the house and leaving her to her fate, are unworthy the name of men.*" (15 p. 501-02)

SCOTT SISTERS
(Guerrillas)

The ladies of Virginia and Maryland showed themselves to be, as a rule, fiercer in the secessionism than the men. By their aid, many a disaster was brought upon the Union cause and the ... officers and men engaged in it's defense.

In the summer of 1861, two young ladies of the name of Scott, residents of Fairfax County, VA, were the means of capturing the Captain of a volunteer regiment from Connecticut. They were at last taken themselves ... by [the trickery of] a scouting party who were earnestly in pursuit of the two in question. ~~Quoted (24 p. 563)

SARAH EMMA EDMONDS SEELEYE

SARAH EMMA EDMONDS SEELEYE
aka Franklin Thompson
(Soldier - 2nd Mich, Co. F)

She was borne Sarah Emma Edmonds, in New Brunswick, Canada - 1841, the youngest and only girl among six children. As a child, she worked alongside her brothers on the family farm. Later, to keep her close to home, her father, [Isaac Edmonson], arranged a marriage for her with an old farmer. Her mother [Elizabeth Leeper], however, assisted her in running away to the United States where she became a Bible salesman and first adopted her disguise as Franklin Thompson.

With the advent of war, and her whereabouts having been discovered by her father, Sarah attempted to enlist, having been inspired by the story of a female in disguise as a sailor (**Fanny Camp**, see **ELIZABTH TAYLOR**). She failed her first physical because she was too short - only 5'6" when the requirement was 5'8 1/4". She was successful on her second attempt, and enlisted with her good friend William Morse in the Flint Union Greys on May 14, 1861, stating...

"It is true I am not American ...not obliged to remain here during this terrible strife ...But it is not my desire to seek personal ease and comfort while so much sorrow and distress fill the land." She felt her disguise as a man would make it easier to *"... perform the necessary duties for sick and wounded men, and with less embarrassment to them ... "* and to herself.

Sarah served with the 2nd Michigan in many major battles such as Bull Run, Antietam and Fredericksburg. At Antietam she buried with her own hands another female soldier in disguise. (See **KILLED AT ANTIETAM**). She served alongside her childhood friend, Lt. James, and as "Frank", she became his best friend - but he never recognized her as Sarah. When he was killed in the Peninsula Campaign, she was devastated and vowed to avenge his death and so - turned from nursing to become a spy for the Union.

She was a master at disguise, even tinting her skin with silver nitrate to become a "black" laborer and cook called "Ned". As a spy during 1862 and 1863, she passed through Confederate lines eleven times to gather information without detection. Fear of being discovered a female, forced her to leave the service in 1863.

In 1864, Sarah wrote her memoirs, "*Nurse and Spy - (Unsexed, the Female Soldier)*" and donated the proceeds from the sale of her book to the care of wounded soldiers. Sarah returned to New Brunswick and fell in love with a mechanic named Linus H. Seeleye. He followed her back to the United States in 1866 and they were married in Oberlin, OH, on April 27, 1867. They had three children.

In 1884 she attended a reunion of the 2nd Michigan. Her former comrades were at first shocked to discover her a woman and then seeing her poor physical condition, encouraged and supported her in applying for a pension. Sarah was awarded a veteran's pension of $12 a month, but it was not until 1886 that the 49th Congress removed the term "deserter" from her official records. (Nat'l Archives - Pension Record #SC282,136)

In 1891, Sarah's son, Frederick, married and moved to La Porte, TX, where Sarah and Linus joined he and his wife and spent the rest of their days. She was soon in contact with her former comrades who lived in the Lone Star State and in 1897 was mustered into the George B. McClellan Post in Houston, thereby becoming the only woman member of the Grand Army of the Republic.

Sarah died a year later at the age of 57, on Sep. 5, 1898. She was buried near LaPorte, but her remains were moved on Memorial Day 1901 to the G.A.R. plot of Houston's (then called German Cemetery) Washington Cemetery with full military honors. She is the only woman buried there and her tombstone reads: "Emma E. Seeleye, Army Nurse".

The following is an incident from Sarah's memoirs as soldier, Franklin Thompson:

SENT OUT TO PROCURE SUPPLIES, Sarah dismounted at the house of a Southern woman, whose dress indicated she was in deep mourning. Invited inside, she kept an eye on her horse as the woman prepared the goods. Feeling she was deliberately being detained, Sarah urged the woman to complete her task quickly.

The woman was pale and nervous as she handed Sarah the basket of food, and refused the money Sarah tried to give her in payment. So, she thanked her, and left. After having ridden only a few yards, the woman shot at Sarah, but missed. Sarah wheeled her horse and drew her revolver.

The woman fired a second time, again missing her mark. As Sarah prepared to fire back only to wound, the woman dropped her pistol and imploringly raised both her hands. Sarah deliberately shot her through the palm of the left hand, upon which, the woman fell to the ground in a screaming faint.

Tying her by her right wrist, Sarah dragged the woman a short distance along the ground to rouse her - upon which, she begged Sarah to let her go. Instead, Sarah took her prisoner and set out for McClellan's headquarters. As they travelled, they began to talk and Sarah discovered that in the last three weeks, the woman had lost her father, husband, and two brothers. Her attack on Sarah had been spurred by her overwhelming grief and anger, as Sarah had the misfortune of being the first Union soldier the woman had seen since the triple tradgedy.

The woman told Sarah that if she would not take her before the military, she would take the oath of allegiance and become a nurse for the Union. The agreement made, neither ever told how the woman's hand was injured. Only that she was shot by a yankee. The Confederate woman went on to become one of the most faithful and qualified nurses to the Army of the Potomac. (12),(17),(26),(29)

MARY SEIZGLE
(Soldier - 41st NY)

According to Moore's, *"THE REBELLION RECORD"*, Mary impersonated a soldier and served with the 41st NY.

SHERIDAN'S DISCOVERY
(Two Soldiers - 15th MO)

The memoirs of Gen. Philip H. Sheridan, published in 1888, relate the account of two women who were discovered in his command by Colonel Joseph Conrad in 1863. Evidently, these women had been in the ranks for some time, for Sheridan and some of his men were rather shocked to discover they were women.

One was large and muscular and worked as a teamster on the division wagon train. She was a political refugee from East Tennessee, and had enlisted in Louisville, the year before. The other woman was thought by Sheridan to be "rather prepossessing", and had assumed the identity of a private in a cavalry unit.

Happening across each other, and seeing through one anothers disguise, the women became close friends. They might have lasted for the duration of the war had they not drunk too much "applejack". The two women got quite tipsy, fell into a river and nearly drowned. Their sex was discovered during efforts made to revive them. They were immediately sent to headquarters, put in dresses, and sent home. (23)

MARY SIMPSON
(Spy, Smuggler, Highwayman)
aka Mary Timms

As four or five citizens of Tennessee were on their way into the interior from Fort Pillow, they were overtaken by a gay and festive woman upon a small sorry looking mule. She rode boldly up to the men, presented a persuader in the shape of a "Colt," and made known her intention of riding her mule no longer, but of confiscating one of their best chargers to supply its place ... but she failed to make her victims fear and tremble. Her violence was not force enough for men who had faced all the dangers of siege and battle, and they rode off, leaving my lady robber alone to her destruction. One of the party, striking into another path, returned to Fort Pillow, and there reported the singular adventure with the woman.

Captain Posten, of the 13th Tennessee cavalry, with a squad of men, was dispatched in pursuit of the bold rider of the little mule. After riding some five miles, she was overtaken near the house of a Mr. Green, and blandly invited to visit the fort - invited in such an insinuating style that she could not find it in her soul to refuse - that is, the pointed arguments used by Captain Posten were more than human logic could fancy or gainsay.

The bold feminine said that no two men could have conquered her, but the numbers overpowered her and she must succumb. She then gave up her arms and was delicately treated by the officer in charge.

Upon being conducted to the fort and properly examined, upon her person were found orders from the rebel Colonel Hicks for a list of contraband supplies, consisting of gunpowder, short cavalry boots, and other articles. On being questioned, she acknowledged she was employed by the rebels in obtaining goods for their comfort and use, and smuggling them through the lines. Her salary was one hundred dollars per month, the rebels supplying the money to pay for her purchases. She usually transacted this business in St. Louis. On the last occasion she had landed from a steamboat at Randolph, and when taken was on her way to the house of a rebel sympathizer.

This female smuggler gave her name as Mary Simpson. At Randolph, she called herself *Mary Timms*, and proved to be a woman well known in the neighboring country, where she had passed under several aliases a year before. She was strongly suspected of being a spy for the rebels and carrying intelligence from Jackson, Tennessee, to the Hatchie. Within a few months, it was found she had proposed to the rebel Colonel Stewart to purchase ammunition for his command.

Mary's age was set down as not far from thirty years, black hair, a brunette complexion, and a deep, dark, penetrating eye. Her intellect quick, and she was not easily disconcerted: and, as her proposed but unsuccessful horse trade with so many of the more masculine sex showed, fearless and dauntless as an ancient highwayman.

She belonged to the married persuasion, her husband being a loyal soldier doing duty for his country at the fort. When she desired to see him after her arrest, he refused; saying she had brought disgrace upon him and their family by aiding the enemies of their country. He only desired that their true names might not be given to the public. The woman refused to tell where the goods were concealed, orders for which she had.~~ Quoted (24)

ALVIRA SMITH
(Scout/Courier - MO)

Alvira was another woman who applied for a pension for her services during the war relative to her activities as scout and courier to the Union in Missouri. (22)

CLARINE ELIZABETH "KINNIE" SMITH

CLARINE ELIZABETH "KINNIE" SMITH
(Courier - C.S.A.)

Born 1844, in Parkersburg, [W] Virginia, Miss Kinnie was only 17 years old when the war broke out, but she was fully devoted to the Confederacy. Many a note concealed in her black tresses was delivered to Southern Officers. Riding twenty miles to carry weapons to a Confederate scout, being instrumental in the escape of seven Confederate prisoners while she was imprisoned in a Wheeling jail, and hiding a treasured Confederate sword from inquisitive foes were among her exploits.

On one instance, a Confederate soldier, home on a foraging trip had just left Miss Kinnie's home when two Federal officers came to her door asking for the soldier. Miss Kinnie told them he was not there, but they searched her house, anyway. As soon as they left, she quickly gathered some of her mother's clothes and started out after the boy, for she knew where he was going.

It was dark, and as soon as she got out of the village limits, she began to run. When she wanted to attract the attention of a soldier she knew, she would give the "Bob White" bird call. When she saw the boy ahead of her, she gave the "Mockingbird" call which she knew he would recognize as being her call. Not taking the time to answer any of his questions, she began to put her mother's clothes on him, told him to walk like an old lady and get out of that part of the country because the Yankees were after him. Thus disguised, he escaped with his life.~~ Quoted (14 p. 553-54)

[Note: Clarine was a teacher, author, and one of Parkersburg's most distinguished citizens. She died in 1927, and is buried in an unmarked grave in the Odd Fellows Cemetery, Pkbg., WV.

LYDIA SMITH
(Heroine)

J. Howard Wert left behind an account of a totally different kind of hero than the usual stories portray. *"But I promised ... to speak ... of Mrs. Smith ...*

"She belonged to a despised and down-trodden race, for she was a colored woman. She was poor, yet she had a little money saved up, a trifle at a time, by years of labor. Her name was Lydia Smith ... From a white neighbor she hired a ramshackle wagon with which she did hauling, and a horse. The horse was a pile of bones, else probably he would not have been in Adams County at all but mounted by a Confederate cavalryman. Lydia circled widely through the farm section around Bendersville and York Springs, which had not been so utterly devastated as the region contiguous to Gettysburg.

"Eloquently she told of tens of thousands of suffering men: *'I thank de good Lawd that put it into my heart to try to do something for these poor creatures.'* When she could get donations of delicacies and suitable clothing, she accepted them. When donations failed, she bought till she had spent the very last penny of her little hoard acquired by years of frugality and toil.

"But now the wagon was heaped high to its full capacity, and she turned toward the hospitals miles away. The old horse swayed and tottered, but Lydia walked by his side and led him on over dusty highways and rugged hills till, at length, the tents were at hand. And then Lydia, feeling not the weariness from many miles of travel, began to distribute the articles she had brought - to Union soldiers, of course? No! Union and Confederate lay side by side; and that noble colored woman saw not in the latter the warriors who were striving to perpetuate the slavery of her race. She saw only suffering humanity; and to Union and Confederate alike was impartially given the food, the clothing, the delicacies that had been obtained by the expenditure of her last penny." ~~Quoted (11 p. 91-92)

SARAH JANE SMITH
(Saboteur - MO)

Sarah was only fourteen years old when she began her two year adventure of spying and smuggling activities in Missouri. Also acting as saboteur, her greatest offense was that of cutting four miles of telegraph wire in Southeastern Missouri. Her eventual capture in 1864, led to a sentence of death by hanging. Though infamous as an "aggravating nuisance", General Rosecrans commuted her fate to imprisonment instead, for the rest of the war. (22 p. 105)

SOUTHERN CHIVALRY

As confederate Colonel Lander was riding ahead of his troops, and reconnoitering on the way to Phillippi, he came to a house by the roadside where he saw a woman. Yankee-like, he began to question her about the number of secessionists in the neighborhood. She wanted to know what side he belonged to, and he replied by asking if she supposed he would be in that neighborhood if he did not want to join the secessionists?

He learned from her that the rebels had no artillery. Before he returned from his reconnoisance of the town of Phillippi the woman had discovered her mistake, and had a pistol in hand for him, which she discharged at his person, without any damage, however. He took off his hat and bowed to her very gallantly, and begged her not to shoot at his men, as they would kill her.

Just then the advance of his reconnoitering party came up, when he ordered a couple of them to seize the woman's son, a lad of about seventeen, to prevent him informing the enemy of their approach. The boy was immediately seized, when the mother came at them with an axe and the fury of a savage, and they had to let the boy go to defend themselves, when he took to the woods and was soon lost to sight.

As the main body of troops marched by, she fired her pistol at them also, but without effect, her door receiving in return some half-dozen rifleball perforations, to remind her that shooting was a dangerous business.~~Quoted (24)

MRS. STERRITT
(Heroine)

Mrs. Sterritt answered Gov. Cartin's first call and had remained with the Army until Lee's surrender. After the battle of the Rappahannock she heard groans, and although the army was retreating, she stayed to search for them and found a half dozen wounded soldiers hiding, because unable to follow.

These she was having placed in her ambulance when a Confederate officer rode up and called her to halt. Drawing her heavy Colt's revolver, she pointed it full in his face. *"If you interfere with me I'll put a bullet through your head."* She looked as if she would, so the officer, appreciating her courage and resolution, rode away. ~~Quoted -- (*Unidentified news clipping found in old book.*)

BETSY SULLIVAN
(Confederate Vivandiere - TN)

Of the hundreds, perhaps thousands, of women who volunteered to weather the perils of war to serve both North and South, history has recorded few names. The South remembers an Irish lassie named Betsy Sullivan, the wife of a soldier, who served a Tennessee regiment as a cook and laundress. (27)

ELIZABETH TAYLOR
aka Happy Ned
(Sailor)

Enlisted as a sailor, she also became the subject of a popular ballad. (43)

***

NOTE:
See "*Sarah Seeleye*" - In her memoirs, Sarah called herself "Ned" when spying in the guise of a black laborer. Sarah also reported her admiration for a woman named **FANNY CAMP**, who joined the Navy disguised as a male sailor, and inspired Sarah to adopt a male disguise.

MARIA and MATTIE TAYLOR
(Heroines)

Danville, Kentucky, was much divided in allegiance, many who had long been neighbors and friends espousing opposite causes. But there was no doubt as to the sympathies of Mrs. Taylor and her estimable family. Broad and beautiful floated the striped bunting over her cottage, which proclaimed that their hearts, and hopes, and fears were all with the Union cause.

When Kirby Smith occupied Danville, he sent a squad of half a dozen men to take down that piece of bunting from Mrs. Taylor's house. They were met at the door by Mrs. Taylor's two daughters, Maria and Mattie, who politely but firmly announced their intention to resist any effort to remove the national emblem.

The valorous squad returned, and reported that it would require a full company to remove the flag. The force was detailed. A captain marched a hundred men with loaded guns at the door, drew them up in "battle's magnificently stern array," and made a formal demand for the colors.

The young ladies now came to the front door, each armed with a revolver, and holding the glorious banner between them. They replied to the Confederate captain that they had vowed never to surrender that flag, and declared their intention to shoot the first rebel that touched it.

After hesitating a few moments, the officer withdrew his force, and reported that in the exercise of his discretion he had not found it advisable to remove the colors referred to.~~Quoted (15)

SARAH TAYLOR
(Capt. - 1st Tennessee)
Regimental Daughter

One of the features of the 1st Tennessee Regiment, was a brave and accomplished young lady of but eighteen summers and of prepossessing appearance, named Sarah Taylor, of East Tennessee, the step-daughter of Captain Dowden, of the First Tennessee. Miss Taylor was an exile from home, having joined the fortunes of her step-father and her wandering companions, accompanying them in their perilous and dreary flight from their hearths and homesteads.

She formed the determination to share with her late companions the dangers and fatigues of a military campaign; and to this end, she donned a neat blue chapeau, beneath which her long hair was fantastically arranged, bearing at her side a highly finished regulation sword, and silver mounted pistols in her belt, all of which gave her a very neat appearance.

She became quite the idol of the Tennessee boys, who looked upon her as a second Joan of Arc, believing that victory and glory would perch upon the standards borne in the ranks favored by her presence. Miss Captain Taylor was, indeed, all courage and skill. Having become adept in the sword exercise, and a sure shot with a pistol, she determined to lead in the van of the march - to return her exiled countrymen to their homes, if it cost the sacrifice of her own life's blood.

When the order was issued to the Tennesseans to march to reinforce colonel Garrard, the wildest excitement pervaded the whole camp, Miss Taylor mounting her horse cap in hand, galloped along the line like a spirit of flame, cheering on the men. She wore a blue blouse, and was armed with pistols, sword and rifle, and the persecuted Tennesseans looked upon the daring girl who followed their fortunes through sunshine and shadow, with the tenderest feeling of veneration, and each would willingly have offered his life in her defense.

There was but little sleep in the camp on Saturday night, so great was the joy of the men at the prospect of meeting the foe, and at a very early hour in the morning they filed away jubilantly , with their Joan of Arc in the van. Just before taking up their line of march, they all knelt, and lifting up their right hands, solemnly swore never to return without seeing their homes and loved ones. (22) ~~Quoted (24)

MARIE TEBE

MARIE TEBE
aka French Mary
(Vivandiere - 27th PA.Co.I; 114th PA - Collis' Zouaves d'Afrique)

Mary, officially recognized by the military, drew a soldier's pay for over two years, plus 25 cents extra for her work in the hospitals and at headquarters, making a total of $21.25 a month. Her reasons were the same as many other women who followed the war - she refused to be left behind when her husband, Bernardo Tebe - a tailor from Philadelphia, enlisted in 1861.

She first served with her husband in the 27th PA, and then with the 114th PA. Under fire more than a dozen times, she was at Bull Run, Cold Harbor, the Wilderness, Fair Oaks, Richmond, and Spottsylvania's Bloody Angle. She survived Fredericksburg with a wound in the ankle, dashed amid the devastation at Gettysburg, and had her skirts "riddled by bullets" at Chancellorsville.

Like Anna Etheridge, Mary was awarded the Kearny Cross by General Birney for her bravery, but unlike Anna, Mary refused to wear it. (2 p. 6);(28 p. 828)

VIVIA THOMAS
(Soldier)

Vivia was a high-spirited daughter of wealthy Boston parents. She attended Boston society's finest affairs. It was at one of the balls held following the Civil War that Vivia met and fell in love with a handsome young lieutenant. After several months of courtship, their engagement and marriage plans were announced.

Shortly before their wedding date, however, the lieutenant, more intrigued by Vivia's wealth and place in society than by her beauty, suddenly left. The note he wrote to Vivia stated he desired to go West in search of adventure, that marriage and Boston society were not for him.

Broken-hearted and bitter over the embarrassment caused her and her family, Vivia left home in search of her lover. Learning from the military that the lieutenant was stationed at Fort Gibson, Indian Territory, her long journey began. The trip was extremely hard, especially for a girl who had known only luxury. But her vengeful heart pushed her on toward her destination.

She cut her hair, dressed in men's clothing, and joined the military; ... [20 mo.?] She avoided recognition by the young lieutenant, though she frequently observed him. She discovered he had an Indian girlfriend that he visited each evening.

One cold evening in December, Vivia trailed the lieutenant, ambushed and killed him. An intensive investigation was held but to no avail, and the matter was dropped. However, Vivia became remorseful. Disturbed over the killing, she began visiting the grave at night. She contracted pneumonia from the continued exposure and, one night collapsed near her lover's grave. She died shortly after.

A priest Vivia had confessed to, revealed the true story of Vivia. Her comrades were so impressed with the courage it took to come alone into the frontier, and to carry out a successful disguise as a male that, rather than condemning her, they awarded her a place of honor for burial in the "Officer's Circle". Her burial place can be seen at Fort Gibson National Cemetery, Fort Gibson, OK~~Quoted (38)

LUCY MATILDA THOMPSON (Gauss Kenney)
aka Pvt. Bill Thompson, C.S.A
(Soldier - 18th NC, Co.D)
Bladen Light Infantry

Fearing nothing but God and her first husband's death, her motto was:

"Hold your head up and die hard."

In 1861 [about 48 years of age], Lucy had just become the bride of Bryant Gauss, the first man from his section to volunteer. Lucy was not content to wave good-bye. Devoted to Bryant, she feared he would be killed and lie unidentified.

She cut her thick hair close, took up seams in one of Bryant's suits, oiled her squirrel musket and boarded a train for Virginia as Pvt. Bill Thompson. Neighbors and friends sympathized with her bravery. They kept silent. If Capt. Robert Tate of Co. D and Lt. Wiley Sykes knew "Private Bill" was a woman, they kept it to themselves. The secret never went further than company headquarters.

Being an expert sharpshooter mattered most. Besides, she sang well in a husky voice to keep up spirits on long marches in the rain; she took care of the wounded. At first Manassas an iron (shell) scrap tore open her scalp from forehead to crown (she spent 60 days in the hospital and her wound was later protected by a silver plate.) Bryant got wounded three times and finally at the Seven Days near Richmond, (Bennettsville) he was killed. Lucy obtained permanent furlough and took him home for burial.

Lucy was the daughter of Duncan Thompson, believed to be half Indian and of the Waccamau tribe, living between Whitehead and Wilmington, NC. Lucy was borne 21 Nov 1812, a native of Bladenboro, N.C., and lived to be 112 years old!

Her first child, Mary Caroline Gauss, was borne [when Lucy was about 50 years old] Jan. 21, 1864. [Lucy] moved to Savannah about 1866, where she was unknown and from then until 1914 [when she told her pastor] kept her military exploits a secret, not caring for curious questions.

In Savannah, Lucy married her second husband, Joseph Patrick Henry Kenney (6 Apr 1806 - 7 Sep 1913), a street cleaner and Northern veteran. Both she and Joseph were personally acquainted with President Lincoln. [Lucy, at an incredibly mature age, bore Joseph six more children:] They were:

At age 55: 18 Jan 1868, Twins - Martha Glendora and James Duncan Kenney
At age 60: 28 Jan 1873 - Katie Missouri (Kenney) Cason
(Katie had a daughter Martha Cason Wilder, 88 yrs old in June of 1984, Cordele, Ga.; Martha had a daughter, Gloria (Mrs. J.A.)Matthews, 1984, Cordele, Ga.)
At age 63: 19 Apr 1876 - Victoria Elizabeth Kenney
At age 66: 20 Aug 1879 - John P. Kenney
At age 69: 29 Aug 1881 - Joseph Best Kenney
(Great-Grandson Perry L. Streat, Nicholls, GA, 1977)

She came to Georgia after the Charleston earthquake in 1886 and lived in various parts of the state before coming to Nicholls, GA. On her 109th birthday, she gave her views opposing women's suffrage and vividly described her experience during the Charleston earthquake.

Lucy died at the home of her daughter, Mrs. Perry Streat, on 22 Jun 1925, and was buried in the Meeks Cemetery near Nicholls. (39),(44)

THREE WHO DIED
(Soldiers)

A Monroe paper of May 1863, gave the following account: "A Pennsylvania girl who has been living as a soldier in the southwest for ten months, says *she has discovered a great many females among the soldiers*, one of whom is a Lieutenant. She has assisted in burying three female soldiers at different times, whose sex was unknown to anyone but herself." (36) (see: **Frank Martin**)

"TOMMY"
(12th R.I.)

While the Twelfth Rhode Island regiment was on duty in the town of Lancaster, Kentucky, a chubby young Anglo-African, answering to the name of Tommy, came into camp and desired to enter the service of some of Uncle Sam's officers, and was taken by one of the Captains as a body-servant. In this capacity the fugitive followed the regiment through all the experiences and vicissitudes of the campaign, and then home to Rhode Island, always faithful, attentive, cheerful.

But the refinements of civilized life were too much for Tommy, and the Captain's body servant proved to be a veritable daughter of the regiment, - a bona fide girl of less than twenty summers, - who had been able, during all the period of her military service, successfully to conceal her sex in the guise of a boy.
~~Quoted (24)

SALLY TOMPKINS
(Capt., C.S.A)

After the first battle of Manassas it was found that the Confederate government had not provided sufficient hospital accommodations, and a call was made upon private individuals. Miss Sally L. Tompkins volunteered and immediately established a hospital in Judge John Robertson's house on Main and Third Streets, Richmond.

Civil authorities regarded this as irregular as other private hospitals had been placed under the direct supervision of the Confederate Government. Miss Tompkins, however, wanted to maintain her own hospital and seriously objected to giving up what she had so carefully planned at her personal charge and expense.

Though small and frail, Miss Tompkins was determined to continue as superintendent of her private hospital. In the "Old South", it was unheard of to use force to compel a lady to comply with the law, so civil and military powers compromised and granted Miss Tompkins a commission with the rank of Captain. As Captain of Robertson Hospital, she could give herself authority to continue her work and commandeer the services of others as well as whatever official medicines and supplies the Confederate government could afford.

From the first battle of Manassas to June 13,1865, when the hospital closed its doors, she tended over 1,300 sick and wounded soldiers. She was once wealthy, but when she died, over fifty years after Appomattox about 80 years of age, she died in a Home for Needy Confederate Women.
~~Quoted (17)

HARRIET (ROSS) TUBMAN
aka Moses
(Scout, Spy, Heroine)

History has not neglected to record the bravery of Harriet, who - working with John Brown - led many slaves to freedom in the 1840's. What is not so well known is that Harriet never stopped working for the freedom and equality of her race.

Born into slavery in 1821 in Maryland, Harriet was the daughter of slaves Benjamin Ross and Harriet Green. Forced by her master to marry John Tubman, Harriet later married Nelson Davis. She chose, however, to use the name Tubman the rest of her life. She never learned to read or write, but could quote Bible scripture with ease.

Escaping from slavery while still a teenager, it is reported that over the next ten years she made nearly twenty trips to the South and led more than three hundred slaves to freedom, including her parents. On these journeys Harriet felt it necessary to carry a revolver, and on at least one instance was forced to turn it upon one of her fellow refugees. The exhausted slave had demanded to stop for a rest and refused to go any further. Harriet, fearing the danger this would impose on the entire band, pointed her revolver at the laggard and threatened, *"Dead niggers tell no tales. You go on or you die."*

Harriet's fame was widespread by the time the Civil War erupted and she was called on by Governor Andrew of Massachusetts to assist the Union Army as scout and spy. He sent her to South Carolina where she was attached to the army as a cook and laundress under General David Hunter. During this service, she was to lead many successful raids and gathered much valuable information for the North.

Even after the war, her efforts never ceased. Among her many lifetime accomplishments were the establishment of many schools in the South, and a home for the aged in Auburn, New York, where she died in 1913, at age 92. (23)

MADAME TURCHIN
(Officer's Wife - 119th IL)

Madame Turchin, the wife of the Colonel [later, Brig. Gen.] of the 19th Ill., [a wealthy Don Cossack named John Basil Turchin - Russian name, Ivan Vasilievitch Turginoff], was the daughter of a Russian officer, and was born [26 Nov 1826, Russia] and reared in foreign camps, a favorite with the men of her father's command. [She and her husband came to the United States after the Crimean War.]

In the Spring of 1862, when the 19th Ill. was actively engaged in Tennessee, Colonel Turchin was taken seriously ill, and was carried for days in an ambulance. Madame Turchin not only nursed her husband most tenderly, but took his place at the head of the regiment - the men in the ranks, and the subordinate officers, according her implicit and cheerful obedience.

She was not one whit behind her husband in courage or military skill. Utterly devoid of fear, and manifesting perfect indifference to shot or shell, or minie balls, even when they fell thickly around her, she led the troops into action, facing the hottest fire, and fought bravely at their head. When her husband was able to resume his command, she gave herself again to the care of the sick and wounded, in the field hospital.

[Another illness for her husband occurred during the Atlanta campaign that ended both their military careers. They went home to Kenwood, IL., a suburb of Chicago, and worked together as immigration agents for the Illinois Central Railroad. Later, they moved to Radom, IL., where they established a colony of Polish immigrants, and spent the last of their days.]

[The General died in 1901, but Madame Turchin was refused a pension and was forced to live on the charity of the men of his brigade. Eventually, she was granted a pension of $50 a month. She survived her beloved husband only a few years, and died on 17 Jul 1904.]~~Quoted (16);[23]

TWO PRISONERS FROM GEORGIA
(A Soldier and a Prostitute)
Sherman's XX Corps and
the 33rd Indiana

Sherman's memoirs recount the incident of the burning of the prison at Milledgeville, GA. The fire was set by women prisoners, who used the occasion to escape.

At least two of the escapees attached themselves to the military. One, a convicted murderer, joined the XX Corps, and the other - in the male guise of a soldier - plied her "ancient trade" in the camp of the 33rd Indiana. (21)

TWO TENNESSEE WOMEN
(Heroines)

During the Autumn of 1862, when Grant was commanding in West Tennessee with headquarters at Jackson, the 27th Iowa was ordered to take the cars at Corinth and proceed to Jackson.

It was night time and the train was crowded, men occupying the platforms and covering the roofs of the cars. As he approached a bridge, the engineer saw two lanterns in the distance swung to and fro with the greatest earnestness. He gave the signal of danger; the brakes were instantly applied, the train stopped, and men sent forward to ascertain the cause of the alarm.

Two women were found at the bridge, who said the coming of the loaded train of Union soldiers was known to a gang of guerrillas which infested the neighborhood. In the early part of the night the assassins had fired the bridge, and allowed the string-pieces to burn nearly off, when they extinguished the fire, and left the structure standing, but so weak that it would go down as soon as a train came over it.

Hearing of this piece of dastard villainy, the women had left home in the dead of night, and travelled on foot several miles through the woods, to give an alarm and prevent the fearful consequences that would otherwise have ensued.

The officers and men whose lives were thus saved begged of these heroic women to accept a purse of money, which was made up on the spot. This they refused; and all the return they would permit was that small squad of the soldiers might see them safely home. ~~Quoted (15)

ELIZABETH VAN LEW
aka "Crazy Bet"
(Union Spy)

In Stockhoe Cemetery, Richmond, a marker reads, "*She risked everything that is dear to man - friends, fortune, comfort, health, life itself...*" It is the grave marker of "Miss Lizzy", as she was called to her face - or "Crazy Bet" as she was referred to behind closed doors.

Even Richmond papers were so bold as to imply that she and her mother were sympathizers and acted as spies for the Union, though the papers rarely referred to them by name. Local officials were familiar, however, with the eccentric antics that earned Elizabeth the nickname "Crazy Bet", and therefore paid no heed to the insinuations of the press. They considered her crazy - but harmless - and left her alone.

Due to her convincing performances and the unconcerned attitude of officials, she was able to move about freely and thereby became one of the most effective spies of the war. (22)(28)

LORETA VELASQUEZ

LORETA JANETA VELASQUEZ
aka Lt. Harry T. Buford, C.S.A.
(Soldier - 21st Louisiana)

Loreta is perhaps one of the most controversial soldier women of the Civil War. In 1867, she wrote a book about her experiences (most of which some feel are contrived) entitled: *"The Woman in Battle: A Narrative of the Exploits, Adventures, and Travels of Madame Loreta Janeta Velasquez, Otherwise Known as Lieutenant Harry T. Buford, C.S.A."*.

In this work, she claims to have been blockade runner and spy, and fought as a soldier in major battles. In her male disguise, she had access to high officials - even the Presidents - of both North and South.

The general consensus was that she exaggerated her experiences and capitalized on the sensation of her book in order to support herself and her baby. Ex-Confederate General Jubal Early was known to be her harshest critic. It is the opinion of others, however, that such a book would have been impossible to write at the time, unless it was based on an element of fact. How much is true? Were they her experiences only, or a combination of her own experiences with those of other women she knew in the field?

In the 1990's, with so many volumes having been written on every facet of the Civil War including it's women, it is not unreasonable to assume that there is some factual basis for her book. How much is fact and how much is fiction, is not known. The exploits of **MADILINE MOORE** and **ELSA GUERIN** have been suspect in the same light, but who can know for sure ?

Lest anyone be tempted to doubt that there have been women active at the front in every war (discernible or not), the following fact should first be considered: - the hand that rocks the cradle, will stop at nothing to protect the babe that sleeps therein.

Loreta was Spanish, born in Havana, Cuba in 1842, and educated in New Orleans. Seeking to turn her life into an adventure, she eloped in 1856 with an Army officer, Capt. Thomas DeCaulp, who died only three weeks after they married.

She married again, for she states that her husband refused to let her follow him to war. Not to be stopped, she proceeded to go to great lengths to disguise her femininity - a wire frame to flatten her curves, a false mustache, a Confederate officer's uniform, and the name of *Lt. Harry T. Buford.*

She recruited a company of volunteers in Arkansas, trained them in New Orleans and led them to Pensacola in 1861, where she turned them over to her amazed husband who furthered their training. It was during this training that a carbine exploded in her husband's hands, killing him instantly. She was devastated by his death and turned all her efforts toward the military.

She claims to have participated in the battles of 1st Bull Run, Ball's Bluff, and Fort Donelson ... that her sex was discovered in New Orleans in the Spring of 1862, so she fled, and as Harry, enlisted in the 21st Louisiana. She reports having been wounded at Shiloh, which again revealed that she was a woman; after which she continued as a sometimes male, sometimes female spy. Loreta married a third time and eventually bore four children. (9) (13)(27) (ref: C.J. Worthington, *THE WOMAN IN BATTLE*)

VIVANDIERE
(Defined)

The literature presented by the United States Army Military History Institute at Carlisle Barracks, Pennsylvania states...

"Laundresses, prostitutes, female combatants, and other camp followers, including wives, were often collectively referred to as vivandieres, whether they fit the definition or not. ... That women accompanied Civil War soldiers into the fields with their regiments is an historically established fact."

The word `vivandiere' comes from a 12th Century combination of French and Latin words for food, and in the 15th Century was defined as `hospitality giver'. Webster's 3rd New International Dictionary Unabr., defines `vivandiere' as *"a woman formerly accompanying troops to sell provisions and liquor to soldiers; a female sutler."*

Vivandieres first appeared in French army camps in the 1600's - evidently in great numbers - and were regulated in 1653 to four per regiment of ten companies and twelve per regiment of thirty companies. The cavalry was afforded one per regiment. Further regulations in 1778 allowed the women one horse. Evidently the numbers of women appearing in the camps grew to great numbers for in 1793, the only women who were permitted in camp were the laundresses and canteen keepers.

By the 1800's, the clothing of canteen women had become more military in style. The semi-uniforms that evolved were officially recognized as they often incorporated the style and colors of the men in their regiments. This evolution to military dress came about due to necessity, as women's clothing was scarce and inadequate in the field.

It was in 1854 that the term `vivandiere' was officially changed to `cantiniere', though the former term is used more often in historical reports of our Civil War. By 1860, the uniformed women were officially recognized and afforded the same privileges, pay, and honors as their male counterparts with whom they marched. No less than six cantinieres accompanied the 39th New York, and five marched off with the 25th Pennsylvania. Of the hundreds of official cantinieres attached to the Union army, there were those who returned home after realizing the dangers of war. The South was not without its own cantinieres too, as noted throughout this manuscript.

During the Civil War, these vivandiere/ cantinieres were given yet another name, that of Daughters of the Regiment, or Regimental Daughter. It is nearly impossible to separate these women by title or duty as they performed in multiple capacities - from a beloved mascot such as little **LIZZIE JONES**, to the armed and fearless nurses and color bearers such as **ANNA ETHERIDGE** and **KADY BROWNELL.**

It goes without saying that this was the vehicle by which women were permitted to participate in an acceptable capacity, and without having to disguise their sex. However, once the flood gates were opened, every woman inspired by Joan of Arc and looking for an adventure - regardless of motive - answered the call. This is evidenced by the fact that in 1865, after the Civil War, another regulation was issued limiting cantinieres to two per light infantry battalion, two per cavalry squadron, and four per artillery or engineer regiment.

In Farrow's Military Encyclopedia, Vol.I, page 282, and Vol. III, page 570, both `vivandiere' and `cantiniere' are defined. The major difference being that the `cantiniere' was officially recognized where the `vivandiere' wasn't, even though they both performed the functions of sutler.

Bearing all this in mind, it is still difficult to know which few of the ladies within these pages were "officially" recognized, and which of those (who represent the majority), were not. It should certainly shed some light, however, as to why there are so few references to these women in our history books. (2) (27) (28)

SARAH ROSETTA WAKEMAN

SARAH ROSETTA WAKEMAN
aka Lyons/Edwin Wakeman
(Soldier-153rd NYSV,Co.G&H)

"I don't know how long before I shall have to go into the field of battle ... I don't believe there are any rebel bullets made for me yet. Nor I don't care if there is. If it is God's will for me to fall in the field of battle, it is my will to do and never and never return home." --Washington, Aug. 5, 1863

Similar sentiments were expressed by tens of thousands of Civil War soldiers in their letters and diaries. In fact, after reading the letters this particular soldier wrote home during his service from 1862 to his death in New Orleans in 1864, most historians would judge him to be a typical soldier of the period. But this soldier was far from typical - "he" was a woman named Sarah Rosetta Wakeman who enlisted under the assumed name and male identity of "Lyons [and Edwin R.] Wakeman".

Sarah Rosetta Wakeman was buried in New Orleans along with her secret. She remains a man on her service records.[~~Quoted Article, by Lauren Cook Burgess; *References*: War records and Sarah's unpublished letters home.]

Imagine the excitement more than 100 years after her death, when Sarah's descendants discovered a chest containing many of her letters, as well as an old daguerreotype of Sarah in uniform as "Lyons R., Edwin R., or S. R." Wakeman, and some of her personal belongings! Later, her war records were discovered under the name of Lyons Wakeman.

Between family and war records, we know that Sarah was born on 16 Jan 1843 in Afton, N.Y., the first of the nine children born to Harvey Anabel and Emily Hale Wakeman. Sarah's father was a farmer and sometimes carpenter. [Two of Sarah's sisters were named Susan, who died in 1876, and Sophronia, who died in 1937. According to descendant nephew Burl A. Wilder, his grandfather [perhaps Perry Wilder] was married to Susan and later to Sophronia.] There is no record of Sarah having been married.

Sarah, described as being only five feet tall, had a fair complexion, blue eyes and brown hair. She ran away from home and worked on the Chenango Canal from Binghamton to Utica. At nineteen, on 30 Aug 1862, she enlisted for three years at Roots, NY (near Fonda, Herkimer Co.) stating her occupation as "boatman/coal handler". She enlisted in the 153rd NYVI, Co. G (later Co.H), and received $152 for enlisting - which she sent home to be used for food and clothing for her family.

Sarah served in the Washington area until 14 Feb 1864, before being shipped to New Orleans. She took part in several engagements with the 153rd no doubt including the Red River Campaign, for her last dated letter home on 14 April 1864, was from Brandycore Landing, LA and states, "Made advance up the river about 40 miles to Pleasant Hill - had a fight. Retreated 10 miles, next day the fight resumed at 8:00." In her final undated letter she said they expected to go to Mobile.

In a letter home 3 Sep 1863, she tells of having Guard duty at "Cairol Prison", and in an undated portion of a letter states the following -

"Over at Cairl Prison they have got three women that are confined in their rooms. One of them was a Major in the union army and she went into battle with her men. When the rebels bullets were a-coming like a hail storm she rode her horse and gave orders to the men ... The other two are rebel spies ... smart looking ... good education." (See: **Rose O'Neil**)

Upon her death, the ring Sarah wore, inscribed inside with her real name "Rosetta Wakeman, NY Vol. Co. H, 153rd", was sent home and later discovered with her letters. According to her service records, she was hospitalized 7 May 1864, as case #6747 (for chronic diarrhea) in the Marine U.S. Army General Hospital in New Orleans, where she died a few weeks later on 19 Jun 1864, and was buried the same day in Grave #17, Monument Cemetery. In 1939 the War Department gave over the administration of this cemetery to the National Park Service and it is now known as Chalmette National Cemetery, Chalmette, LA, with Sarah's grave being #4066, Section 52.

Medal of Honor Recipient
DR. MARY WALKER

DR. MARY WALKER
(Surgeon - 52nd OH)

AWARDED THE
Medal of Honor

No account of the contributions women have made to American history would be complete without mention of this remarkably dauntless, and eccentric advocate of women's rights - especially in the field of medicine.

Born Mary Edwards Walker on 26 Nov 1832 in Oswego, NY, she was teaching in her parents' school by the time she was sixteen. By the time she was twenty three she had received a medical degree from Syracuse Medical College and had begun private practice both in Rowe, NY and Columbus, OH.

The advent of trousers for women, made famous by Mrs. Amelia Bloomer paved the way, however, for a stigma that would forever overshadow Mary's brilliant career, for Mary chose to wear pants. Her "uniform" eventually evolved to a combined version of the semi-uniforms worn by some women and already described herein, and a suit of men's clothing. No doubt she adopted this form of dress for the same reasons the other women did - practicality and comfort in adverse conditions. Add the fact that she practiced in the male dominated field of medicine, and the result was that she was considered a "freak". Mary married a fellow-physician, but after they separated , she chose to use her maiden name for the rest of her life.

At the time the Civil War began, Mary was twenty nine years old and immediately abandoned her practice to enlist as a Union surgeon. She was refused the commission because of her sex, so she served at the front as a nurse for three years. She was among those who aided the thousands of sick and wounded from Fredericksburg and Chickamauga. During the latter, her work was finally recognized by General Thomas, who ordered her to report as the regiment's Assistant Surgeon. She was finally on the Army's payroll - but denied an officer's commission.

In January of 1864, Mary wrote to President Lincoln, telling him of her service, and of the problems she had encountered because of her sex. While waiting for some response, she was captured April 10, on a battlefield in Tennessee and spent four months in Libby Prison and exchanged in August.

On October 5, 1864, she was notified of her commission as First Lieutenant and Asistant Surgeon at $100 a month. She also received $432.36 for past services. Although she made and wore an officer's uniform, no one would officially recognize her as such. After the war was over, Mary never ceased her efforts to obtain official recognition and wrote letter after letter to President Johnson demanding she be recognized. Instead - she was given the **MEDAL OF HONOR.**

Mary's life appears to be one of constant quest and distress. She retired from the army in June of 1865, with a pension. She worked for a while at a New York newspaper, then went back into medical practice in Washington. But she was constantly being harassed and criticized for wearing trousers, even to the point of being arrested. And she wore her medal every day.

The crowning blow to Mary's entire career and contribution was to fall in 1916, when Congress redefined the standards for granting the Medal of Honor - to require "combat with the enemy". As a result of this new ruling, hundreds of Medal of Honor recipients, including Mary, had their awards revoked.

Unstoppable Mary - at eighty four years of age - went off to Washington to appeal to Congress. While there, however, Mary fell on the steps of the Capitol. Injured, she went home to Bunker Hill, NY, and suffered from those injuries until her death in 1919. Mary never lived to see her Medal reinstated. There are those people, however, who are outraged at injustice and who - some way, someday (even if it takes sixty years) - will see to it that a wrong is righted.

The wrong done to Dr. Mary Walker was righted on June 10, 1977, thanks to the efforts of one of her descendants, when the Army Board of Correction of Military Records, reinstated her Medal of Honor, on the grounds that she should have been commissioned in 1861, but was denied because she was a woman. (2)(8)(12)23)

WARRIOR RIVER
(Two Young Heroines)

Near Warrior River, two young girls - they were seventeen and eighteen - poorly but neatly dressed in homespun and with bare feet, appeared leading three accoutered horses and driving before them three Union soldiers. Each of the girls bore a shotgun on her shoulder. They delivered their captives to [N.B.] Forest, and asked permission to go forward with the Southern troops; but they were satisfied - rather they were delighted with gift of two horses. ~~Quoted (19)

WHO WAS SHE ?
"Woman Confederate soldier a mystery."
-- *National Tribune*, Jul 10, 1902

(** **Author' Note**: In some instances I received sources of information too late to quote, regarding other accounts of women in the ranks, so have merely noted them in this volume for your reference.)

LAURA J. WILLIAMS
aka Henry Buford
(Soldier - C.S.A.)

A comparison of the accounts of Laura against those of LORETA VELAZQUEZ, would appear to suggest that they are one in the same. (32)

ELIZA WILSON
(Vivandiere - 5th Wisconsin)

At twenty years of age, Eliza was a much respected member of the 5th WI. Like many other "Daughters", she served in this unit along with several other members of her family. The daughter of wealthy mill owner and former member of the State Senate, William Wilson of Menomonie, Eliza was afforded her own private tent and servants.

But true to the calling of the vivandiere, her duties were "*to head the regiment when in parade, and to assuage the thirst of the wounded and dying on the battlefield.*" These duties this gentle, pretty girl carried out faithfully, and the soldiers loved her.

Despite her father's wealth and position, Eliza was uniformed as officially set down by military order for nurses, called the Turkish costume. The uniform consisted of a bright brown calf-length dress under which she wore "bloomers" of the same color, gathered at the ankle, and tucked into her gaiters. She wore no petticoats. At times she wore over her dress, a dark brown frock coat with loose fitting sleeves and buttoned it tightly at her waist. Her shoes were morocco boots. She wore a black hat with a black feather plume. It was reported that she was still with the regiment in January of 1862, but that she had been quite ill. (20) (22), also: *Wisconsin Women in the War*.

FANNY and NELLIE

FANNY WILSON and NELLIE GRAVES
(Soldiers - 24h New Jersey, 3rd IL Cav.)

Miss Fanny Wilson [19] was a native of Williamsburg, Long Island, and about one year prior to the war she went to the West, visiting a relative who resided at Lafayette, Indiana. While there, her leisure moments were frequently employed in communicating by affectionate epistles with one to whom her heart had been given and her hand had been promised before leaving her native city - a young man from New Jersey.

After a residence of about one year with her western relative, and just as the war was beginning to prove a reality, Fanny, in company with a certain Miss Nellie Graves, who also had come from the East, and there left a lover, set out upon her return to her home and family. While on their way thither, the two young ladies concocted a scheme, the romantic nature of which was doubtless its most attractive feature.

The call for troops having been issued, and the several States coming quickly forward with their first brave boys, it so had happened that those two youths whose hearts had been exchanged for those of the pair who then were on their happy way toward them, enlisted in a certain and the same regiment. Having obtained cognizance of this fact, Fanny and her companion conceived the idea of assuming the uniform, enlisting in the service, and following their lovers to the field.

Their plans were soon matured and carried into effect. A sufficient change having been made in their personal appearance, - their hair cut to the requisite shortness, and themselves re-clothed to suit their purpose - they sought the locality of the chosen regiment, offered their services, and were accepted and mustered in.

In just another company from their own, of the same regiment - the Twenty-fourth New Jersey - were their patriotic lovers, 'known though all unknowing.' On parade, in the drill, they were together; they obeyed the same command. In the quick evolutions of the field they came as close as they had in other days, even on the floor of the dancing school; and yet, notwithstanding all this, the facts of the case were not made known.

But the Twenty-fourth, by the fate of war, was ordered before Vicksburg, having already served through the first campaign in Western Virginia; and here, alas for Fanny, she was to suffer by one blow. Here her brave lover was wounded. She sought his cot, watched over him, and half revealed her true sex or nature in her devotion and gentleness. She nursed him faithfully and long - but he died.

Next after this, by the reverse of fortune, Fanny herself and her companion were both thrown upon their hospital cots exhausted and sick. With others, both wounded and debilitated, they were sent to Cairo. Their attendants were more constant and scrutinizing. Suspicion began to be excited - the discovery of Fanny's and Nellie's true sex was made.

Of course the next event in their romantic history was a dismissal from the service. But not until her health had improved sufficiently was Fanny dismissed from the sick ward of the hospital. This happened, however, a week or two after her sex had become known.

Nellie, who up to this time had shared the fate of her companion, was now no longer allowed to do so; her illness became serious, she was detained in the hospital, and Fanny and she parted - their histories no longer being linked.

Having again entered society as a member of her real sex, Fanny was next heard of on the stage of a theater at Cairo, serving an engagement as a ballet girl. But this was for only a few days. She turns up in Memphis, even as a soldier again! But she had changed her branch of the military service, having become a private in the Third Illinois Cavalry. Only two weeks, however, had she been listed in this capacity, when to her utter surprise, she was stopped by a guard and arrested for being a woman in men's clothing.

She was taken to the office of the detective police and questioned until no doubt remained as to her identity, not proving herself, as was suspected, a rebel spy, but a Federal soldier. An appropriate wardrobe was procured her, and her word given that she would not again attempt a disguise.

A brief description of Fanny would be that of a young lady of about nineteen years, of a fair but somewhat tanned face, rather masculine voice, sprightly and somewhat educated mind - being very easily able to pass herself off for a boy of about seventeen or eighteen years. ~~Quoted 24 p. 170-71; (20 p. 49);(22 p. 80); and *Frank Leslie's Illustrated Newspaper*, 7 Mar 1863.

MAGGIE WILSON
aka Charles Marshall
(Soldier - 13th NY)

"...one of the 13th Regiment's men, a pale-faced youth named Charles Marshall, turned out to be Maggie Wilson (1861) She stayed on as a vivandiere.." [Ref. Unknown at this time - *Courtesy E. A. Livingston*]

MARY WISE
(Soldier - 34th Ind. Vol.)

Claiming two years' service and wounded, three times, Mary received pay for this service before being mustered out. (22 p. 80) and *New York Herald,* 14 Aug 1864

ANNIE WITTENMYER

Annie, author of "Under the Guns", Stillings & Co., Boston, 1885, became the patron saint of the thousands of women who gave so selflessly during the Civil War. Thirty years after the war, its rigors had taken their toll on these women and many were sick and destitute. They appealed to Annie to use her influence in Washington to obtain some kind of compensation for their services.

So, on their behalf, Annie went to Washington and lobbied for five months to get a bill passed that would grant these women some relief. A bill was passed that would grant each woman twelve dollars a month if she could prove she gave service during the war.

Some women did receive compensation of six or ten dollars a month during the war years they served, but records were poorly kept and of very little use in proving their claims. It is impossible to know how many died in extreme poverty and without any recognition at all "despite the fact that the civil war soldiers were more indebted to these women than to any other class of people." (7 p. 389)

WOMEN OF CASTROVILLE

In order to defend themselves against Indians while the men were away fighting in the war, the women of Castroville, Texas, organized themselves and began to drill with guns and pistols. (27)

WOUNDED AT CHICKAMAUGA
(Soldiers)

There were several reports of soldier women being wounded at Chickamauga. Annie Wittenmeyer reported in her book "*Under the Guns*" that she had befriended a captured 26-28 year old woman (who's home was in the Northwest) in the hospitals at both Chattanooga and Nashville. Annie convinced the young woman to divulge her name and address so she could be sent home, but the young woman who'd served as a Private for more than a year, swore Annie to secrecy.

In another report, a captured, wounded woman was returned to the Union by the Confederates with a note stating: "*As the Confederates do not use women in war, this woman, wounded in battle, is returned to you.*"(5)   (See: **Frances Hook**)

WOUNDED AT GETTYSBURG
(Soldier)

In a letter written by a wounded Michigan man from the U.S. Military Hospital in Chester, Pennsylvania, this interesting account emerges. *"I must tell you we have got a female secesh here. She was wounded at Gettysburg, but our doctors soon found her out. I have not seen her, but they say she is very good looking. The poor girl has lost a leg. It is a great pity she did not stay at home with mother but she gets good care and kind treatment. But it is rather romantic to have a female soldier in the hospital and her only to have one leg and far away from home, but I hope she will soon get better and get home to her friends."*~~Quoted (10)

WOUNDED WOMAN YANK
(Soldier - Indiana Cavalry)

The attitude of male Yanks toward comrades disclosed as women was usually one of amused tolerance. A typical comment was that of a Hoosier cavalryman who wrote his wife in February, 1863:

"We discovered last week a soldier who turned out to be a girl. She had already been in service for 21 months and was twice wounded. Maybe she would have remained undiscovered for a long time if she hadn't fainted. She was given a warm bath which gave the secret away." -- Indiana Cavalryman, to his wife, February 1863 (1)

I AM NOT ACCUSTOMED TO USE THE
LANGUAGE OF EULOGY.
I HAVE NEVER STUDIED THE ART
OF PAYING COMPLIMENTS TO WOMEN.
BUT I MUST SAY THAT, IF ALL THAT HAS BEEN SAID
BY ORATORS AND POETS SINCE THE CREATION OF THE
WORLD
IN PRAISE OF WOMEN
WAS APPLIED TO THE WOMEN OF AMERICA,
IT WOULD NOT DO THEM JUSTICE
FOR THEIR CONDUCT DURING THIS WAR.
I WILL CLOSE BY SAYING,
GOD BLESS THE WOMEN OF AMERICA.

--ABRAHAM LINCOLN

BIBLIOGRAPHY

ANDREWS, Matthew Page, *WOMEN OF THE SOUTH IN WAR TIMES*, Norman Remington, Balt. (1920) *[17]*

ANTHONY, S.B., *HISTORY OF WOMEN'S SUFFRAGE* Rochester, NY (1881-1889) *[36]*

AUSTERMAN, Wayne R., *"Lock & Load, Miss Scarlett"*, (Per.) SO. PARTISANS, FALL '88 *[32]*

BEAR, Henry C., *CIVIL WAR LETTERS OF ...* Lincoln Memorial Univ. Press, TN (1961) *[41]*

BOATNER, Mark M.,III, *CIVIL WAR DICTIONARY*, David McKay Co., Inc., NY (1959) *[28]*

BOOTH, Sally Smith, *WOMEN OF '76*, Hastings House, NY (1973) *[25]*

BOSLO, *SOLDIERS and SAILORS TALES OF THE REBELLION*, Vol. 1, No. 12, (1868) *[40]*

BOTKIN, B.A., *CIVIL WAR TREASURY*, Random House (1960) *[29]*

CHANG, Ina, *A SEPARATE BATTLE*, Lodestar, Div. of Penguin Books, NY - (c) by Laing Communications, WA (1991) *[20]*

CIVIL WAR BOOK EXCHANGE and *COLLECTORS NEWS* Jul/Aug 1987/1989 *[39]*

COCO, Gregory A., *ON THE BLOODSTAINED FIELD*, Vol. I, Thomas Publications, PA (1987) *[10]*

COCO, Gregory A., *ON THE BLOODSTAINED FIELD, Vol. II*,
Thomas Publications, PA (1989) *[11]*

COPELAND, Peter , *CIVIL WAR COLORING BOOK*,
Dover Publications, Inc., NYC (1977) *[12]*

COX, Samuel S., *UNION-DISUNION-REUNION*,
Three Decades of Federal Legislation 1855-1885,
J.M. Stoddard & Co., Wash.D.C., (1885) *[31]*

DANNETT, Sylvia, *NOBLE WOMEN OF THE NORTH*,
Sagamond Press, Tho.Yoseloff, NYC, (1959) *[7]*

DAVIS, Burke, *SHERMAN'S MARCH*
Random House, NY (1980) *[21]*

DIVIDED WE FOUGHT, McMillan Co., NY (1952) *[34]*

DEVENS, R.M., *PICTORIAL BOOK OF ANECDOTES OF THE REBELLION*
(Frazier Kirkland, pseu.) J.H. Mason, Pub. St. Louis, MO (1889) *[24]*

HALL, Richard, *PATRIOTS IN DISGUISE*
Paragon House, NY (1993) *[44]*

HERGESHEIMER, Joseph, *SWORD & ROSES*
Alfred A. Knopf, NY (1929) *[19]*

JOHNSON, Rossiter, *CAMPFIRE and BATTLEFIELD*
Civil War Press, NY (1967) *[30]*

KELLER, Allan, *MORGAN'S RAID*
Bobbs Merrill Co., Sub. of Howard W. Sams &
Co., NY (1961) *[6]*

LIVERMORE, Mary, *MY STORY OF THE WAR*
A.D. Worthington & Co., CT (1890) *[16]*

LONN, Ella, *DESERTION DURING THE CIVIL WAR*
Peter Smith, MA (1966) *[26]*

LONN, Ella, *FOREIGNERS IN THE CONFEDERACY*
Peter Smith, MA (1965) *[27]*

MASSEY, Mary E., *BONNET BRIGADES*
Alfred A. Knopf, NY (1966) *[22]*

MATHENY, H.E., *WOOD CO. W.VA in the CIVIL WAR TIMES*
(c) Joseph M. Sakach, Jr., Trans- Allegheny Books, WV *[14]*

MAZULLA, Fred, *MOUNTAIN CHARLIE*
Univ. of Oklahoma Press (1968) *[37]*

MINERVA QUARTERLY, Spring 1990 *[43]*

MILITARY UNIFORMS & WEAPONRY - The Poster
Book of the Civil War, Military Press,
Crown Publishers, NY (1987) *[4]*

MILLS, H. Sinclair, Jr., *VIVANDIERES*
CW Historicals, Collinswood, NJ *[2]*
(**Wendy King's** *"CLAD IN UNIFORM"* also available
from this publisher.)

MOORE, Frank, *WOMEN OF THE WAR*
S.S. Scranton & Co., Hartford, Conn., Pub.
by National Pub. Co., OH (1866) *[15]*

OWEN, Wm., *IN CAMP & BATTLE WITH WASHINGTON ARTILLERY* ,
M A (1885) *[35]*

RICHARDSON, Albert D., *THE SECRET SERVICE*
American Publishing Co, OH (1865) *[18]*

SIFAKIS, Stewart, *WHO was WHO in the CIVIL
WAR*, Facts on File Publications, NY (1988) *[13]*

TRUBY, J. David, *WOMEN AT WAR*
Paladin Press (1977) *[42]*

TRUDEAU, Noah Andre, *BLOODY ROADS SOUTH*
Little, Brown and Company, MA (1989) *[33]*

TRUESDALE, Capt. John, *THE BLUECOATS*
Jones Bros. (1867) *[3]*

US NEWS and WORLD REPORT, Special Edition
MEDAL OF HONOR Issue, Sep 15, 1991,US NEWS
& WORLD REPORT, INC., Washington DC (1991) *[8]*

VETERANS ADMIN., *FLORENA BUDWIN*
Ft. Gibson Nat'l Cem., OK *[38]*

WARD, Geoffrey C., *THE CIVIL WAR*
   Alfred A. Knopf, Pub., NYC (1990) *[5]*

WILEY, Bell Irvin, *THE LIFE OF BILLY YANK*
   Louisiana State Univ.Press, LA(1989) *[1]*

WILEY, Bell Irvin, *THE LIFE OF JOHNNY REB*
   Louisiana State Univ.Press, LA (1989) *[9]*

YOUNG, Agatha, *THE WOMEN AND THE CRISIS*
   McDowell,Oblensky, NY (1959) *[23]*

* * *

"Hearts of Fire"

Reenactor's Addendum

The Reenactors

Emilie Boneham ... 199
Lauren Cook Burgess ... 204
Bernadette Claudio ... 207
Beth Delene Cowsert ... 211
Dianne Drewes ... 214
Allison Ehlert ... 217
Susan Hindle ... 221
Eleanor Hoffman ... 225
Wendy King ... 228
Sharon Raines ... 231
Sandra Smith ... 234
Beth Anne Stuart ... 236
Cyndi Sunshine ... 239
Patricia Anne Willis ... 245
Catherine Hunter Wise ... 249

INTRODUCTION

[Note: Since there are no Civil War soldier women surviving today and few first-hand accounts existing to draw upon, the main purpose for including this addendum was an attempt to gain some idea of what the women who actually disguised themselves as men in the ranks might have experienced. The next best thing we might do, is talk to some of the women who reenact these situations; but without being in a life-threatening confrontation, it would seem impossible to imagine. However, each reenactor was asked the same questions (including the difficult and / or exciting events they've personally encountered) and it is interesting to study the differences in their responses.

In addition, this addendum might act as a brief and very elementary guide to those who may have an interest in Civil War reenacting roles for women.]

Women's Roles in Civil War Reenacting

Each year, Civil War reenacting gains in popularity as a dedicated hobby as well as a lingering tribute to those who fought and died in the war that would change our country forever. More and more men and women are finding reenacting an interesting and serious, yet exhilarating experience.

For those who participate, as well as for those who observe, it is an exciting way to spend a weekend, an opportunity to meet new friends, but more importantly - a brief escape into the living history of a time passed. Both educational as well as entertaining, reenacting is a form of recreation that can involve the entire family, for there are roles that children can portray as well, in both the military and civilian aspects.

Those in military dress are primarily men, where the majority of the civilian segment is made up of women and children. The most acceptable and commonly known avenue by which a woman could take a more stimulating role without disguising her sex, would be to assume the role of a battlefield nurse. There were many nurses on and near the battlefields of the Civil War. Volumes have been written about brave nurses - such as Clara Barton - and therefore would be easy to research.

Further, a woman might portray an Officer's wife, as they often accompanied their husbands from camp to camp - sometimes bringing their children, as well. Because the Civil War was fought in our own back yards, nearly every military encampment had its "camp followers", comprised of soldier's wives and children, tainted ladies, merchants, photographers, laundresses, cooks, clergy, tavern keepers, undertakers, reporters, etc. Some were highly respected and welcome, while others were looked upon with disdain, depending on how they conducted themselves. These civilian camps were usually set apart from where the soldiers were camped, and in some instances, became little cities in themselves.

Apart from the most acceptable woman's role as a civilian "lady" or a nurse, there are lesser roles a woman might choose, but which will require in-depth research to recreate those roles authentically.

The key word among most reenactors is AUTHENTICITY. Like anything else, however, "authenticity" can be carried to extremes, and those who carry it to extremes have thrown cold water on the enthusiasm of a potentially new reenactor. Therefore, you might want to attend several reenactments and talk to those who are already involved. Most will be more than willing to talk with you and answer your questions. Some will treat you like an intruder. But don't give up.

If portraying a Victorian "lady", nurse, or wife is too tame for you, you might choose to assume a more aggressive role as a spy, courier, scout, guerrilla, saboteur, mail-runner, musician, or color-bearer. Many of the Civil War women who actually participated in these ways, took whatever measures necessary to carry out their missions. Most were well armed, athletic, and good riders. If you choose such a role, however, be prepared to meet with a lot of opposition as these are not commonly accepted women's roles in reenacting - even though women acted in this capacity during the actual war. *It should be especially noted, however, that the average age range of these women was mid-teens to mid-twenties!*

Although these ladies no doubt numbered in the thousands back in the 1860's, many reenacting groups reject these roles in the 1990's. If one of these roles is your ultimate goal, you will have a better chance if you are able to prove your character is authentic. Even having done all that, they may still reject you. Many events/units have a "No women in uniform" ruling.

Even more obscure would be the role of a "Vivandiere" and/or a "Daughter of the Regiment". Although simply defined, a vivandiere (or cantoniere, i.e.- canteen) was a sutler or laundress, where a daughter of the regiment would be more like a "mascot" - possibly a family member of someone in the unit, or a favored, orphaned child as was Lizzie Jones.

Both groups were recognized by the government and wore a variety of fanciful, handmade "semi-uniforms", which did not disguise their female gender. There were so many, both North and South, that after the war the government set a fixed number as to how many could be attached to the military.

In the materials available for research, it is difficult to separate vivandieres, nurses, and regimental daughters. In many cases (like Kady Brownell), women served in *multiple* capacities. Although women served in great numbers, the more aggressive roles are the most difficult to research for authenticity.

The ultimate reenacting challenge would be to portray a woman who disguised herself as a man and enlisted as a soldier to fight within the ranks. Those who were able to keep their identities hidden for any length of time, weathered all conditions, perils and regimens to become every bit a soldier. Their numbers and scope of reasonings for their impersonations have already been explored within these pages; nevertheless, they could ride and shoot and fight - and did. Yet, upon discovery of their sex, most were put into dresses and sent home.

Unfortunately, few of these "soldier-women" were recognized or pensioned by the Government, nor was their participation recorded for history. Most of those who were able to pull it off, obviously took their secret to the grave. Remember, these were *Victorian* times and impersonating a man would ruin a lady's reputation.

In this addendum, you will meet a few of today's "semi-soldiers" and "soldier-women", who share some of their experiences in reenacting. To the women herein interviewed, reenacting is more than just a pleasurable step back in time; there is no doubt that they share an emotional *kin-ship* to the women of the 1860's.

- L.M. 1993

EMILIE BONEHAM

EMILIE BONEHAM

aka "Emil Klem"

EMILIE BONEHAM

aka Emil Klem

(Trooper - 9th NY Vol. Cav.)

Reenactor

Barely in her teens, young Emily has been reenacting with her family for a year. She is the only soldier woman in her unit, and chose her name as a combination of her first name and an ancestral surname.

As an eighth grader, Emilie saw "Glory" in class, and her interest in the Civil War was borne. With the encouragement of her family, she and her little brother both wanted to participate. So dad ordered a dress for Emilie and a uniform for her little brother. But when the clothes arrived, the uniform was too big for her brother, so guess who got the uniform!

Emilie's determination was put to the test when her father challenged her to successfully convince the *VERY AUTHENTIC* 9th NY, that she was her brother! *"I had to fool the men into thinking I was a boy, just like they had to in the Civil War."*

After cramming the two feet of hair she had left (after cutting off eight inches) into a bummer, trimming her neck and sideburns, and slipping into the too big uniform, Emilie says she looked just like "Jonah" in the book, "Hard Tack & Coffee".

When she was introduced, she withstood the usual jibes a young boy would receive and was dubbed the "runt". But they never suspected she was a girl. She knew for sure she had them convinced when later, in formation, some "Rebels" walked by and commented that it would be easy to take "that boy" a prisoner - until she pulled her Colt Army 44 on them. Alas, however, another girl recognized her and told others, so by the end of the day, everyone knew. She says the men were surprised and amused, but no one got mad.

In civilian costume, Emilie portrays a spy.

Emilie's most exciting experience was the first day at Gettysburg, and is best told in her own words: *"I was overwhelmed with the emotions of battle. I was so excited and my adrenaline was pumping. The rows of Confederates kept marching on us and though we dropped some of them, they had our Cavalry hopelessly outnumbered. I fired everything I had and then the Rebs charged, killing all the men beside me. I thought I had a single round left in my 44 and I fired as a Reb came charging at me. He was only five feet away and I would have gotten him, but the gun misfired and powder flew all over my hand and the Reb would have gotten me.*

One of the Union guys on my right was also out of ammo, but threw himself on the Reb, taking him down. He was shot dead and then I took a hit because the Rebs were all over the unit. I saw dead and wounded Rebs and Yanks all around me as I lay still (dying) I even groaned for effect. Then, about ten minutes later, the battle ended and the crowds cheered. I never had such a thrilling experience in my life!"

LAUREN COOK BURGESS

aka "Larry"

LAUREN COOK BURGESS

aka "Larry"

(Musician - 21st GA Vol. Inf., 53rd PA, 18th NC)

Reenactor

Lauren became interested in Civil War reenacting when her husband "literally dragged" her to Gettysburg Battlefield Park three years ago. After observing for about a year, Lauren - who has played the flute for 25 years - and her husband became fully active. They attend 15 to 20 major events each season.

Lauren plays fife in the field music and chose the role of a private so that she could carry a musket. She says there is one other woman in her Georgia unit.

On the problems women may encounter by assuming a male role in reenacting, Lauren is practically an expert. The story of her law suit against the National Park Service for expelling her from an event has made national news.

But to Lauren, every event she attends is a rewarding experience for her, and especially at events where her fife and drum unit are featured. Each member has 50 to 400 tunes memorized, including all the camp duties, like reveille, etc. They are very popular with the crowds.

Lauren feels that she is well accepted within her own unit and with those who know her as something more than "*that woman who is suing the Park Service.*" She's easy going and "*can march till the cows come home.*" Lauren's advice for women interested in arms-bearing reenacting is:

"***Do EVERYTHING you can*** *to sport the best male impression you can - cut your hair short rather than putting it up in your cap; bind your chest; if you can't speak in a husky voice, don't talk (or keep it monosyllabic; be* **MORE authentic** *with your uniform and kit than the most authentic male reenactor in your unit;* **STUDY** *Hardee's or Casey's tactics so you know the drill better than your pards;* **READ MORE HISTORY** *than your pards and* **KNOW IT!** *In short, just like every other non-traditional occupation that women undertake, you're going to have to be ten time better than the men to be accepted and appreciated.*"

~~~~~~~~~~~~~~~~~~~~~~~~~~~~~

BERNADETTE CLAUDIO

BERNADETTE CLAUDIO

in uniform

BERNADETTE CLAUDIO

(Pvt. 124th NYSVI)

Reenactor

In private life, Bernadette is a Licensed Practical Nurse and a Firearms Instructor. Civil War reenacting seemed like the natural thing to do. After observing their first event, she and her husband were "hooked".

To Bernadette, reenacting is a very special form of recreation. *"Just to be able to do something as exciting as Civil War reenacting, together with my husband and friends! Where else can you escape 130 years into the past, relive history, and come away with a new and better understanding of what it was like back then?"*

Bernadette's problems with her impersonation as a soldier have been few. She feels that the efforts and expense to which she has gone to equip herself and blend in with her filemates has gained her much respect in the ranks. In her unit, when one member is not welcome at an event, none from their unit attends - and they inform the sponsors as to why they are not attending. She feels that *"a girl in the ranks is more authentic than a guy in designer sunglasses!"*

She advises, *"Look and be the part. You must be able to blend in. Otherwise, you will not be able to do honor to the soldier women of the 1860's."*

BETH DELENE COWSERT

in civilian costume

BETH DELENE COWSERT

in uniform

BETH DELENE COWSERT

(Private - Rockbridge Artillery)

From Havre DeGrace, MD, Beth has been reenacting with her mother for over a year. She became interested when she met some friends in a fabric store who invited her to a party. Beth participates in 13 major events, 3-4 balls, and 2-3 parades each year.

One of the hardest things for Beth in her portrayal is to reenact alongside her boyfriend - a Captain. She finds it hard to treat him *man-to-man*, and to avoid touching him as a woman would. She tries to keep plenty of distance between them.

Beth's pleasures come from being able to look at a cannon and identify it, and to be able to say, *"I was there - I was a powder monkey - I blew those Yanks apart!"*

DIANNE DREWES

aka "Dan"

DIANNE DREWES

aka Dan

(Private - 124th NY, Co. A)

Reenactor

Dianne is an art teacher who specializes in watercolor, and pen and ink drawings. Her primary interest in Civil War reenacting came about through her desire to take photographs for later sketches. She has been reenacting about three years and attends seven or eight major events, plus parades and educational presentations.

Like some of the other reenactors interviewed here, she feels her most rewarding experience was just being accepted. She feels too, that women draw undue attention to themselves by arriving in female apparel, and then changing into a uniform! They are less effective because everyone knows ahead of time that they are women.

Her best advice to you is to be serious, don't complain, and don't do anything to call attention to yourself. She feels that some of the reasons women went off to fight in the Civil War might have been for the excitement of stepping out of the "norm", and of course out of patriotism. She adds, *"I think most problems were avoided by being quietly reclusive. It must have been a lonely life."*

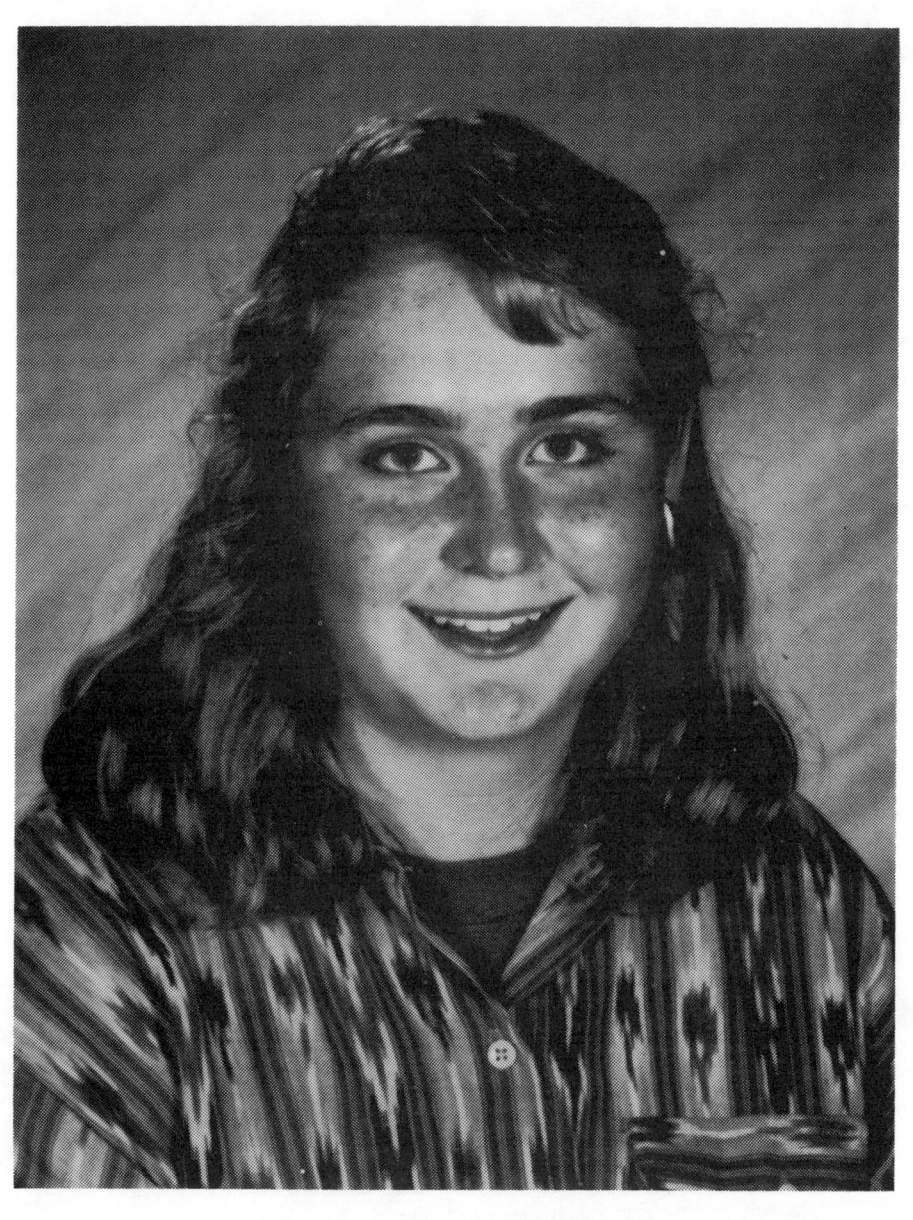

ALLISON EHLERT

ALLISON EHLERT

in uniform

ALLISON EHLERT

aka Private Ehlert

(Soldier- 69th NY VI)

Reenactor

Now eighteen years of age, Allison has been reenacting alongside her father and sister since she was twelve. She currently portrays a male Union musician, and plays the fife.

Initially, Allison (an Ohio resident) became interested through her father who was a member of the NSSA (North-South Skirmish Association). Her fondest memory was when she and her family participated in the 125th Anniversary of Gettysburg.

Allison's greatest rewards are the new friends she makes at each event. Of concern to her is the racial prejudice she's witnessed, more so than any sexual discrimination she's experienced. Her most memorable disappointment was being prohibited from joining a desirable unit because of her sex. The unit had a drummer and she felt it would have been an excellent combination of fife and drum.

To anyone who is interested in reenacting, Allison encourages, "*Give it a try!. it's fun, and an educational experience - a great way to meet people!*"

SUSAN C. HINDLE

SUSAN C. HINDLE

aka "Pvt Sam Wesley-Hindle

SUSAN C. HINDLE

aka Pvt. Sam Wesley-Hindle

(Soldier - 1st Minn. Vol.)

Reenactor

Susan has been reenacting in England for fourteen years. She is forty seven years old and participates with other members of her family. She is one of two female soldiers in her unit of forty four.

In 1979, when she first became interested in reenacting, she read everything she could get her hands on, being very little in England in those days. She was told by those she approached that she could be a nurse or a civilian, but she wanted to be a soldier.

She first reenacted as a gunner, but after detection as a female, she was permitted to be a drummer. Working harder at her disguise, she eventually outfitted herself with various uniforms so she would be prepared for any chance that presented itself for her to participate.

In 1989, a group of Americans attended an event at Leighton Hall in the North of England. The friendships she formed made it possible for her to visit the United States and join them for a five week tour of the Eastern Theater.

After many years of disappointments in England due to the "no women on the field" ruling, fellow members and various officers campaigned vigorously to have the ruling changed so that it would allow women "at the discretion of the commanding officer". The motion was carried in November, 1990. Not only did they ask her to encourage other women soldiers, but was told she is often used as an example of how women should present themselves when in disguise as a man. *"Difficult"*, she states, *"because you must train yourself to be on guard at all times NOT to think, talk, act or look like a woman in disguise."*

Susan feels that women who do not disguise their shape, or remove their make-up, nail polish and earrings, make it more difficult for everyone else to be taken seriously.

The highlight of her reenacting experiences has been her trip to the United States, and she plans to return again in 1992. In everyday life, Susan is a part-time delivery driver and also acts as a sutler, sewing and constructing Civil War clothing.

ELEANOR HOFFMAN

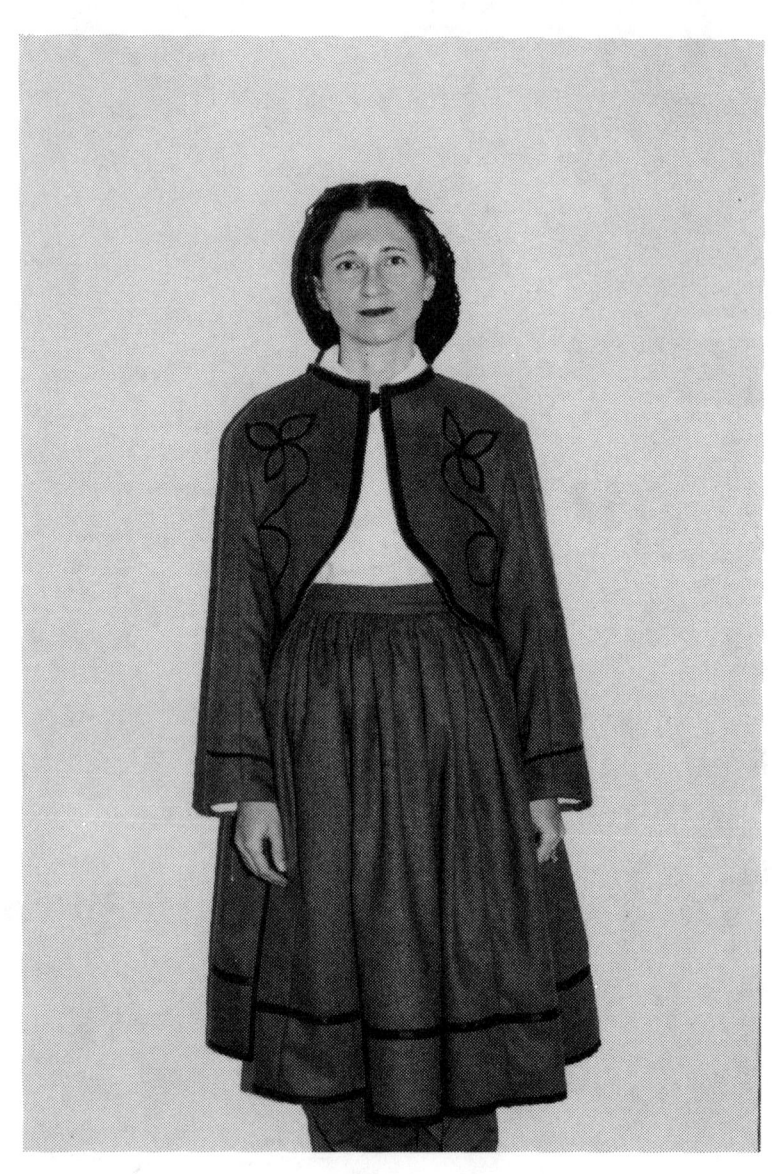

ELEANOR HOFFMAN

in Vivandiere costume

ELEANOR HOFFMAN

(Vivandiere/Nurse - 1st MD Inf)

Reenactor

A resident of the state of New York, at thirty seven years of age, Eleanor is relatively new to reenacting. She has chosen her role because it gives her an active opportunity to educate the public. Interested in the Civil War since high school, along with a love for the theater, reenacting was the perfect combination. Once decided, she found her greatest obstacle to getting involved was finding a unit that would allow women.

Eleanor is currently the official unit musician, playing the guitar, but is also learning to play the fife, and has given lectures on Civil War medicine.

A most memorable experience for Eleanor was at an event where she portrayed a lady from Baltimore trying to find her missing brother who had run off to join the Confederacy. She approached some spectators with a "carte de visite" (photo) of her "brother", and asked if they'd seen him. The young child in the group was wide-eyed and took it very seriously, turning to her mother to say, *"Mommy, is she really looking for him?"*

WENDY A. KING

aka "Craig Anderson"

WENDY A. KING

aka Craig Anderson

(Soldier - 2nd VA Inf.)

Reenactor

Wendy, a resident of West Virginia, is 31, married, and has been reenacting for seven years. Her husband is also involved in reenacting. They were married on Jan. 25, 1992, in a 19th Century atmosphere, complete with gowns, uniforms and all!

Wendy chose to portray Craig Anderson because she likes the excitement of being "in the thick of it". She feels the traditional women's roles are too tame, as she has always been a physically active person. Originally Wendy disguised herself to portray a soldier in Revolutionary War reenactments.

Wendy reenacts with both the 2nd VA Inf., Co. and 26th Va. Btn., Co. G. She is the only female soldier in the 26th, and shares the role with another female soldier in the 2nd.

Enjoying her hobby to the utmost, her most rewarding experiences have occurred when her disguise has gone undetected - to the surprise of her comrades when she dons feminine apparel after an event.

Despite the controversy regarding women who portray men, Wendy feels that over 70% of those who know she is a woman accept and even encourage her in her role. She has had only one "official" problem with discrimination. Her greatest frustration is with those who refuse to accept the fact that her portrayal as a female in disguise is historically accurate.

Wendy advises those who would attempt such a role as she plays, not to use "half measures" in your disguise. The hair, especially, must be convincing, as well as binding of the chest. She adds: *"Follow the orders, learn the drills, and practice, practice, practice!"*

When asked her observations of some of the problems Civil War soldier-women might have faced, she was quick to note the problems involved with relieving bodily functions when in camp and in the field. She cites it can be especially embarrassing when confronted by a personal situation in which a male comrades is not aware of her sex. She simply states, *"I just look the other way."*

In Wendy's own recently published booklet *"Clad in Uniform: Women Soldiers of the Civil War"*, she notes circumstances that may have made it easily possible for women to remain undetected. Most being the fact that living conditions varied drastically, uniforms were poorly fitted, and controls were often extremely lax.

SHARON RAINES

SHARON RAINES

in uniform

SHARON RAINES

(Fifer - 28th MA)

Sharon was introduced to reenacting by her children who play fife and drum, and together they attend all the major events. She has had no encounters with her portrayal and enjoys it immensely. Her greatest pleasure is when people tell her how much they enjoy the music. She is very close to the members of her corps as two are her sons and the others she has watched grow over the last five years.

She is disturbed about the attention the subject of female soldiers is receiving, and it makes her uncomfortable. She says she felt like people were *looking* for women, just to make an issue of it. She personally has had no problems. She states, *"I take the role seriously ... and try to cover myself the best I can."*

Sharon feels women of the 1860's took their roles seriously, too - ***"They were willing to die for it."***

SANDRA SMITH

aka "Sam/Sandy"

SANDRA SMITH

aka Sam/Sandy

(Private - 71st PA Inf. Co. A)

Reenactor

A Librarian, Sandra is relatively new to reenacting and chose her role as a soldier to help educate the public on this missing piece of history. Once she had researched the subject, she set about to find a unit who would accept her.

Other than a few jeers from other units at first, she has been well received and enjoys carrying her impersonation further to the public through speaking engagements.

She encourages the new reenactor to "*be an asset - it helps also to be able to play an instrument, as they like the music.*" Sandra plays the violin and recorder. She also points out the importance of showing up at as many events as you can - "*be part of the group - don't hang on the fringes or it opens you up to criticism. And last but not least .... **let the boys be boys!***"

BETH ANNE STUART

in her father's uniform

BETH ANNE STUART

(Sgt. - Maryland Signal Detachment)

Beth began reenacting with her father off and on in 1961. After his passing in 1978, she chose the Infantry to honor his memory. Her father joined the 53rd VA for 1st Manassas in 1961. She now wears his uniform and carries his musket. Beth attends nearly one event every week of the year!

Her biggest problem was finding a unit that would take her permanently. Many would let her join them for the day, but not on a full time basis, until the Signal Detachment.

Working as a Middle School Health and Physical educator, Beth loves learning new skills, and being part of a champion musket team. (Funkstown, 1991).

Beth emphasizes, *"Fit in ... learn to be a real soldier ... don't draw attention to yourself."*

CYNTHIA A. SUNSHINE

CYNTHIA A. SUNSHINE

aka "Frank Thompson"

CYNTHIA A. SUNSHINE

aka Frank Thompson

(Soldier - 1st NJ Cav Vol Rgt)

Mifflin Guard, PA

Reenactor

Serving the United States Army since 1984, Cyndi chose to portray the character of Sarah Emma Edmonds Seeleye in reenacting. Although Sarah served with the 2nd Michigan, Cyndi's portrayal is in honor of Sarah's service to the Union.

Cyndi has been reenacting for seven years and recalls her most rewarding memory when, *"after the 125th Gettysburg battle, everyone who participated got down on one knee and prayed for those who came before us, while two buglers from opposite ends of the field played "taps" - a beautiful and emotional moment."*

At Cyndi's first reenactment she was told, *"If you want to play with the boys, you will be treated as one of the boys."* Her fellow troopers are of the general opinion that a woman should not participate as a soldier, but do not give her a problem so long as she does not use her "feminine gender" to get out of any duties. She says the men really resent those type of ploys, plus the wearing of any type of makeup, however slight.

The most serious problems Cyndi has faced in her reenacting as a trooper is remaining constantly aware of her safety and that of her horse. *"Most horses remain calm under fire, but my horse doesn't like the smoke, noise, yelling and confusion that comes in battle. Added to that is the discomfort of sabres and carbines clanking against their sides, and the additional weight to the saddle of haversack, canteen, blankets, poncho, great coat, rider."*

During her first full cavalry charge (also the horse's) her mount panicked and bolted into an uncontrollable run. Cyndi, thrown off balance due to the additional weight on her person of sabre and carbine, was thrown. As the result of falling on the carbine slung over her shoulder, she broke a small bone in her back and developed and intense fear of the "charge". For a while, she chose instead to portray a "courier", and suffered the brunt of endless good-natured "coward" jokes from other members. Having since conquered her fears, she remains extremely cautious in a charge.

Cyndi is teased a lot by the male members, but they don't deny her the right to participate. Before, during and after an event, she is always called "Frank". Cyndi never reverts to a female role or discloses her feminine gender at anytime during an event - not even in the evening in camp. She portrays her male character at all times in the opinion that this is the most authentic.

Summing up, Cyndi states, *"The Civil War soldier-woman faced not only all of the trials and tribulations as the men, but the additional fears of disclosure and subsequent rape. But, if the will was there to succeed, she did. Some survived the war, some died in battle or from disease, some were discovered and dismissed, some were fined for impersonating a soldier. But their spirit and courage in the face of incredible odds, serves as a constant reminder to those of us who bear arms in their honor that women have and always will play an important part in the history and development of this country."*

PATRICIA ANN WILLIS

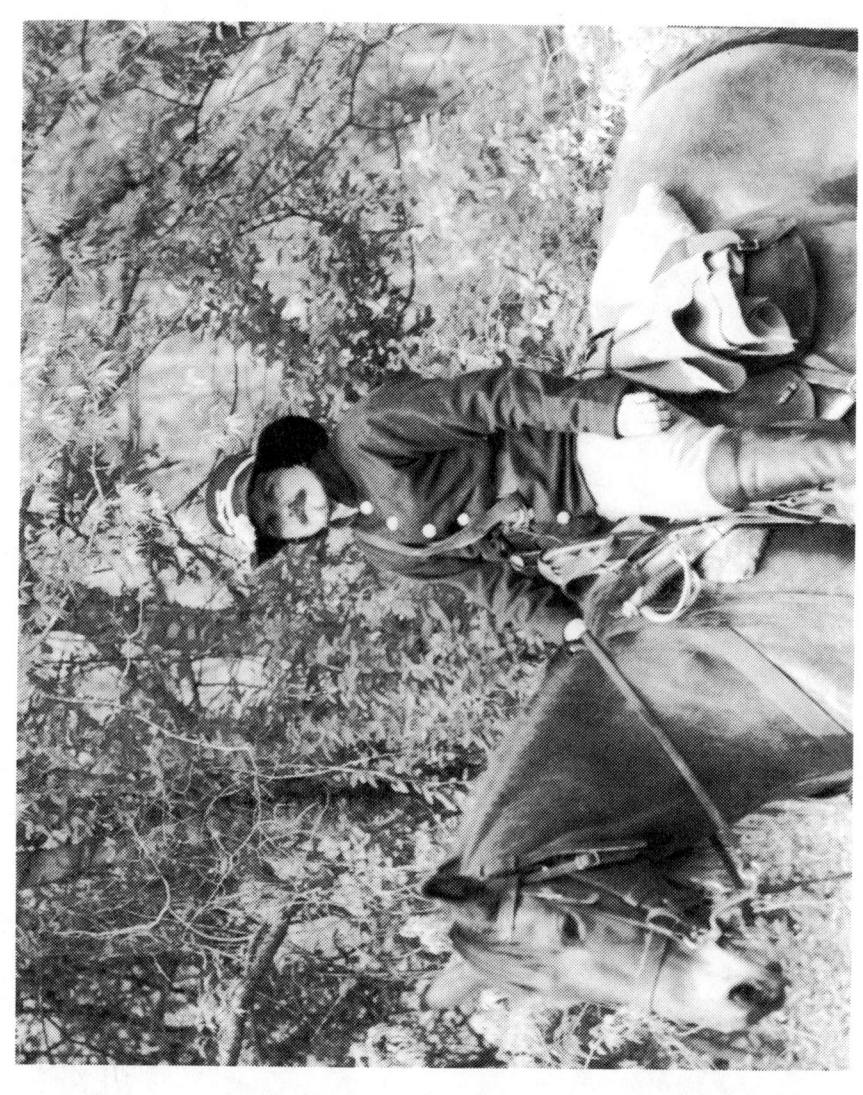

PATRICIA ANN WILLIS

aka "Patrick Willis"

PATRICIA ANN WILLIS

aka Patrick Willis

(Trooper - 2nd GA Cav.)

Reenactor

Forty two years old, married, and a resident of Georgia, Patricia has been reenacting with her husband for four years. Despite her husband's unit's "no women in uniform" ruling, she was permitted to be with him in uniform as a historian/photographer but was left behind during battle. She soon grew bored and left her husband's infantry unit to join a cavalry unit. Soon her husband moved over to be with her. Theirs is a large unit of approximately twenty mounted, plus families.

Excellently disguised in moustache and goatee, combined with "better than average riding skills", she is rarely recognized as being a woman. So convincing is her disguise, that upon occasion she has received un-suspecting requests to escort a "lady". However, severely discriminated against at one event, she and her husband were both ordered off the field. Outraged and embarrassed, they took action to sue. Only after pleas from their friends that it could only cause problems for the whole unit and the events they participated in, did they cease civil action.

Patricia and her husband participated in the filming the Civil War epic "GLORY", and Patty is proud to report that Tri-Star Picture's authenticator told her that she and her horse "looked really good".

Unthreatened by society's rejection of certain "unexpected female behavior", Patricia is not intimidated into hiding the allure which often draws soldiers - male and female - to the "thrill" of battle. To experience the same emotions a man might experience makes her no less a woman any more than a man becomes less a man when he weeps at the first sight of his new born son. Emotions are genderless and one should not be criticized because of them. Her frank summation comes from the heart of someone who has been there, and should not be judged by those who haven't:

"Unless you have experienced a full-blown cavalry charge, down into a valley of smoke and fire ... surrounded by thousands of screaming soldiers ... among the thunder of hooves and booming cannons ... amid the glitter of sunlight on steel ... heady with the scent of a sweating horse under creaking leather ... tasted the adrenalin coarsing through your veins to deposit it's taint on your tongue ... you can't imagine what happens inside you. Because, for just a few fleeting moments, the years fall away and you are there - its the 1860's - and you're riding hard with Jeb and Bobby Lee."

CATHERINE HUNTER WISE

CATHERINE HUNTER WISE

aka "Hunter Wise"

CATHERINE HUNTER WISE

aka Hunter Wise

(Trooper - 43rd VA Cav.)

Reenactor

Cathy, 34, a resident of Georgia, has been a horsewoman all her life. She was "hooked" after she saw her first reenactment, and admits she is living out a fantasy of *"riding a noble steed and doing great battle with a fine blade."*

Her mount, "Count of War", is a five year old thoroughbred gelding which she broke and trained herself. Cathy is a riding instructor and trainer of race horses. She has just completed a technical book on horses and soon hopes to make a full career change to writing.

Cathy effects her disguise by wearing a moustache and sideburns, and tucks her waist-length hair up under her cap. To hide her feminine voice, she takes advantage of a scar on her throat to portray a mute cavalryman.

Her advice to women interested in assuming a male role, would be that they not attempt to "out macho" the men, or create an issue of being a woman. She states, *"When in uniform, a woman's greatest challenge is to blend into the ranks, perform her duties as a soldier competently, and place the well-being of the unit as a whole above personal politics."* She muses, *"After all, we are not fighting about women's lib, we're fighting Yankees!"*

Discrimination has not been a major problem for Cathy, although the protests of some wives relative to her stepping out of a "traditional" women's role, caused her to be voted out of the first unit she joined. She feels honored that the members of the 43rd solicited her participation, and grateful that they have allowed her to share in the experience.

~~~~~~~~~~~~~~~~~~~~~~~~~~~

#####

REENACTOR'S INFORMATION

Listed below are several periodicals of interest to reenactors. They contain schedules of events, book reviews, articles, units looking for new members, and advertisers who sell Civil War reenactor's clothing, equipment, etc. You will want them all!

CAMP CHASE GAZETTE, P.O. Box 707, Marietta, OH 45750 - *This publication also publishes a handbook for reenactors entitled, "Springing to the Call ... How to Get Started in Civil War Reenacting". It is geared to the male reenactor, but contains a lot of good information.*

THE CIVIL WAR LADY, 622 Third Ave., SW, Pipestone, MN 56164 - *Etiquette, fashion, recipes - for the Victorian lady.*

THE CIVIL WAR NEWS, P.O. Box C, Arlington, MA 02147 - *"For people with an active interest in Civil War History."*

THE COURIER, P.O. Box 1863, Williamsville, NY 14231 - *Something for everyone.*

REENACTOR'S JOURNAL, P.O. box 1864, Varna, IL 61375 - *"Focuses on the real needs of the reenactor ... more information to help you improve your impression whether its military or civilian."*

* * *

LEE TAYLOR MIDDLETON

Lee lives and works in the beautiful and historic Ohio River Valley and is an award-winning, internationally renown Original Doll Artist by trade. Her doll factory in Belpre, Ohio is toured by thousands each year. A Civil War enthusiast, her interests heightened several years ago while researching Civil War records of her ancestors and the fact that she lives along the Ohio River near one of the places through which John Hunt Morgan passed during his infamous raid into Ohio. She has written greeting card verse for American and other greeting card companies, short stories, poetry, and many how-to articles on dollmaking for various magazines as well as edited and published a poetry quarterly. After several years of research, this is her first major work. She is currently working on a Civil War novel, and an autobiography of her dollmaking career.